The Lancaster Baptist Church does not endorse Bible versions other than the King James Version. While we may not support every concept of this book, we feel the contents to be generally helpful for the spiritual reader.

Pastor Jim Townsley

A Heart For The Home:
Biblical help for marriage and child training

New England Baptist Press
1541 West Street
Southington, CT 06489

860-621-6701

Dedication

Bob and Betty Townsley

Dad and Mom, thank you for your humble and sacrificial spirit. Love for your family has always been your greatest priority, second only to the Lord. It is in your honor that I dedicate this book.

A Heart For The Home

Table of Contents

Section One – Marriage

Section Two – Child Training

Appendices

FORWARD

Considering my own frailty, I have endeavored, as much as possible, to rely upon the greatest resource available concerning the home: God's precious Word—the Bible. My purpose in writing this book is not to exalt my knowledge or ability, but to share with you the effectual working of God's grace, in spite of my weaknesses. Any help readers may obtain from the contents of this book ultimately must be attributed to the Holy Spirit.

God is the only expert on the home, but He is willing to guide everyone who will submit to His authority. It would be a great tragedy to read this book and continue a life of stubbornness and self-will. When it comes to building godly homes, *our greatest need is to recognize our great need.*

Where I offer practical suggestions throughout this book, please take them only as suggestions, and not fact. I trust as you read you will receive hope that your home can be a haven of rest that honors the Lord. Herein I hope you find help that is extensive, though it cannot be exhaustive. I trust God will give you a renewed desire to trust and obey His Word. My deepest desire is to see in you a godly "Heart for the Home."

> "I will lift up mine eyes unto the hills, from whence cometh my help. My help cometh from the LORD, which made heaven and earth" (Psalm 121:1-2).

INTRODUCTION

How God Led Me to Write This Book

For more than two years I have been disabled with an incurable voice disorder called spasmodic dysphonia. Losing the ability to speak, turned into a blessing in disguise, however, when God prompted me to write. Although it's been a blessing, writing *A Heart for the Home* has been difficult for several reasons. First, because I had never intended to write for publication, I was not as prepared as I could have been. Had I known that someday I would write a book, I would have been more diligent in my English studies. Second, writing on marriage and child training is a humbling task. As is anyone who has given marital advice, I was sadly lacking in some areas: I recognized right away that only by the Holy Spirit's divine intervention could I succeed in this task. Third, applying truth to practical situations in life is never an easy task. Hearing a great sermon about home life on Sunday morning does not easily translate into change on Monday. Finally, I feared disappointing my Lord.

As I have continued writing, my voice has continued to improve, almost as if I must finish this book, and then my voice will be completely healed. Whether that is true or not, I have renewed energy and enthusiasm to finish this book in a timely fashion, because I believe this book can be a great help to many families.

THE HOME BEGINS AT THE BEGINNING

In the book of Genesis, the book of beginnings, we read of creation. In six days God created the world. Flowers, trees, oceans, mountains, birds and animals; all were created from God's almighty hand. God's creation is more than the human mind can comprehend, but the final day of creation was the pinnacle of His handiwork. On that day, God gathered the dust of the ground and created man, but man was incomplete. Man needed a "helpmeet" (a perfectly matched partner). So God created woman from the man's rib. Together, Adam and Eve, the first man and the first woman, became the first husband and wife. God knew that one woman and one man for life is a perfect plan. If something else were needed, surely God would have created it at this time.

After God finished all His creative works, He beheld His creation and commented that "it was good." Marriage then, is a good thing. There are many good things about marriage, but a few things are paramount:

1. Marriage provides companionship to meet the need of loneliness.
2. Marriage provides emotional support in good times and in bad.
3. Marriage provides fulfillment of godly physical desires.

> "Except the LORD build the house, they labour in vain that build it: except the LORD keep the city, the watchman waketh but in vain. It is vain for you to rise up early, to sit up late, to eat the bread of sorrows: for

so he giveth his beloved sleep. Lo, children are an heritage of the LORD: and the fruit of the womb is his reward. As arrows are in the hand of a mighty man; so are children of the youth. Happy is the man that hath his quiver full of them: they shall not be ashamed, but they shall speak with the enemies in the gate" (Psalm 127:1-5).

EVERY FAMILY NEEDS HELP

Often I have wished I had a reference book on the home, so that when a problem occurs I could research the problem and find an immediate solution. A book containing the solution to every problem would be an instant success and a great help to every family, but the reality is that no such book exists, nor will it ever be written. Building a home is more than an intellectual matter; it involves the emotions and will of every member.

The best I can offer is what I have learned from my experience, study, and training. My desire is that every reader will consider carefully the suggestions and illustrations offered in this book. No one person has all the answers for all family-life situations. I have tried to glean from experienced and successful men and women I have met through the years. I can only pray that the ideas and learning I have gained will somehow help strengthen your home.

Please read this book with an open heart. And as you do, regardless of the shortcomings of this book, I believe you will receive hope and help to strengthen your marriage, guide your children, and build your home for God.

Building a home requires transparency; those who deny their need for help only hinder their progress. Jealousy, anger, and rebellion are ingredients for failure. Admitting the need for help is not a sign of failure, but the gateway to success. The longer I live the more I am convinced of the absolute necessity of God's help in building a strong Christian home.

God designed the master plan for the home, and no one can ever improve God's plan for the family. Every home is intended to be a picture of God and a foreshadowing of heaven. A husband should love his wife as Christ loves the Church, and a wife should submit to her husband as to the Lord. Where proper love and submission exist, the daily interactions in the home will reflect God's personality. All too often, though, a husband or a wife tries to develop relationships only for personal satisfaction or other selfish reasons. We must recognize the importance of our homes in properly reflecting God's glory.

SIN DESTROYS HOMES

Man was created in moral and intellectual likeness to God. Adam and Eve knew only holiness in their home before they committed the first sin. Through Adam and Eve's failure, the first home was so marred by sin that the first child became a murderer rather than a deliverer. The results of sin changed their home from one of holiness to one of strife. Admission of our need of God's help is the first step in the great adventure of making our homes a little heaven on earth.

Many homes are in trouble today. Homes that neglect God have always struggled. Psychology, advice columns, talk shows, and personal opinions from family and friends fall short of God's wonderful plan for the home. Seeking help should begin with God, rather than with the world's counsel. The first step to building a happy home is to recognize that a happy home is not possible unless God Himself does the building. God's plan for your home is that it be a place of security, comfort, and encouragement.

- "Blessed is the man that walketh not in the counsel of the ungodly, nor standeth in the way of sinners, nor sitteth in the seat of the scornful" (Psalm 1:1).

- "Except the LORD build the house, they labour in vain that build it: except the LORD keep the city, the watchman waketh but in vain" (Psalm 127:1).

Section One

MARRIAGE

A Heart For The Home

Chapter One

Precious Memories

I have vivid memories of my childhood, even before my second birthday. Our home, though not perfect, was a place of joy and happiness. Growing up on a small Indiana farm was a wonderful experience. We didn't know we were poor. If fact, in many ways, we were rich. Though we had very little materially, we were happy with what we had.

I recall attending a small Baptist church in Pleasantville, Indiana. After the Sunday morning service my parents and my older sister and I enjoyed big family meals. The gatherings alternated between my grandparents' homes, and often my cousins, aunts, and uncles joined us. Life was simple, but what wonderful times we had. Driving tractors, tending the animals, and building barns and houses were very special activities for me. Although we were not a dedicated Christian family, I treasure my childhood years beyond measure. Now I am thankful that my parents have more than merely youthful memories; Christ is preeminent in their home.

Rearing my own family in the ministry has been equally gratifying. Having my little girls get out of bed and climb onto my lap for breakfast was always a sweet time. Taking the boys fishing, or working around the church or house with them brought personal satisfaction to me and to them. My wife and I are so grateful for these treasured years of child rearing. There were difficulties, but they were always outweighed by the rewards; and I have to confess that I miss those days and special moments.

All our children are now adults; and all, except our youngest daughter who is still in Bible College, preparing for Christian service, are married and serving in the ministry. We now have grandchildren visiting our home. What a blessing it is to have a part in their lives as we endeavor to create memories for them such as those God graciously gave us as children. It is now my children's turn to create a special haven on this earth for their children.

God has a very special plan for the home; and, when followed, His plan results in a wonderful place, with godly parents and loving, obedient children, who are creating precious memories each moment of their lives.

HOMES NEED BIBLICAL HELP

Today's culture is in transition. Despite *how-to* books, seminars, and conferences, many families live in a state of perpetual stress, hostility, frustration, and worldliness. Separation and divorce are destroying many homes, including Christian homes. The sad reality is that, although born-again believers are assured of a blessed home in heaven, few are building happy homes on earth. Having a godly home must be a priority that is identified, chosen, and built with zeal and determination. Success cannot come without effort. Every father must resolve in his own heart to make his home a happy and successful one; and every mother must do the same. A blessed, happy home is never an accident; it's always the result of dedicated parents relying on God's wisdom and strength each moment of every day.

The sad reality is that, although born-again believers are assured of a blessed home in heaven, few are building happy homes on earth.

I realize, of course, that no one is an expert on establishing a Christian home. I have found that, just when I think a problem is solved, something unexpected comes along. Even the best of families have their flaws and weaknesses. Don't listen to self-proclaimed experts who demand that *this is the way it always is*. I have found that *this is the way it always is—except when it isn't*! Just when you think you have it all figured out something will take place to remind you of your frailties. We must seek God's power and wisdom constantly.

God Should Be First

Although I cannot consider myself an expert on the home, I have been blessed to be a husband, father, and now grandfather. My children have been a tremendous joy to my wife and I, as we have watched them mature and serve the Lord. We have tried to keep God first in our home. Before our children were born we determined to make God preeminent in our lives. When I proposed to my wife, I explained to her that she would never have first place in my life because that place belonged to God; however, I also told her she would always have the premier place in my life, above all others except God. She responded, "If God has first place in your life, then I will always be in the highest position possible." That truth has served us well over the years.

Many examples of happy homes can be given. One such home is the well known South African missionary Andrew Murray, who believed that his children served the Lord because they grew up in a home that daily evidenced God's power. He raised eight children to adult life all of whom matured into faithful servants of the Lord. His example is a testimony to all, that children can be trained to serve the Lord.

Several years ago *Christian Life and Faith* magazine presented some unusual facts about two families. In 1677, an immoral man married a licentious woman. Nineteen hundred descendants had come from the generations begun by that union. Of these, 771 were criminals and arrestees, sixty were thieves, and thirty-nine were murderers. Forty of the women were known to have venereal disease. These descendants spent a combined total of 1,300 years behind bars and cost the state of New York nearly three million dollars.

The other family was the Edwards family. The third generation included Jonathan Edwards, the great New England revival preacher who became president of Princeton University. Of the 1,344 descendants, many were college presidents and professors. One hundred eighty-six became ministers of the gospel, and many others were active in their churches. Eighty-six were state senators, three were Congressmen, thirty were judges, and one, Aaron Burr, became Vice President of the United States. Not one was ever known to have spent time in jail or in the poorhouse.

Not all children of good parents become useful citizens, nor do all children of wicked parents turn out bad. Even so, the possibility of a child leading an honorable life is enhanced if he comes from a home where love prevails, the Bible is taught, and prayer is offered.

Christians Can Build Happy Homes

Your spiritual condition does not guarantee that your home life will be a success; however, if you are a Christian, it is possible for you to have a happy Christian home. Often my heart becomes burdened for the homes of many Americans as I observe their obvious mistakes that will certainly lead to heartache. I am sure many of these parents do not realize the dramatic consequences their present mistakes will have on their future—and their children's lives.

Christians must not pattern their homes after the typical American family, but rather, according to the Word of God. The world offers a different paradigm of the family than the Bible does. The Bible teaches that we are to "come out from among them and be ye separate." We are likewise admonished not to be of the world. I want to challenge you to build your home on God's Word and to honor the Lord in your home.

Building a Home Requires Determination and Commitment

Building a godly home requires consistently following biblical principles and faithfully seeking God's will, while obeying His revealed will. We must not forget that marriage was conceived in God's mind before He first instituted it on earth. God's love for the home should be ours as well.

> "And God said, Let us make man in our image, after our likeness: and let them have dominion over the fish of the sea, and over the fowl of the air, and over the cattle, and over all the earth, and over every creeping thing that creepeth upon the earth. So God created man in his own image, in the image of God created he him; male and female created he them" (Genesis 1:26-27).

I have met many people who did not believe their home could be happy. Their spouse or their children somehow seemed to be an exception to the hope of God's restoration. These people assured me they and their family had done all that could be done. It seems many are looking for an excuse rather than a cure; someone to blame rather than someone to forgive. It is always someone else's fault. When we have family problems, we must always look for answers as to how *we may correct our shortcomings*. Blaming God or anyone else must never be an option. Remember, God's promises mean what they say or they mean nothing. We must not blame God or misinterpret His teaching to fit our understanding or compensate for our failures. God means what He says! Every young couple must believe they can have a happy home and raise godly children, based on God's promises. Consider the following promises:

- "Except the LORD build the house, they labour in vain that build it: except the LORD keep the city, the watchman waketh but in vain. It is vain for you to rise up early, to sit up late, to eat the bread of sorrows: for so he giveth his beloved sleep. Lo, children are an heritage of the LORD: and the fruit of the womb is his reward. As arrows are in the hand of a mighty man; so are children of the youth. Happy is the man that hath his quiver full of them: they shall not be ashamed, but they shall speak with the enemies in the gate" (Psalm 127:1-5).
- "Train up a child in the way he should go: and when he is old, he will not depart from it" (Proverbs 22:6).
- "Whoso findeth a wife findeth a good thing, and obtaineth favour of the LORD" (Proverbs 18:22).

THE HEART IS THE KEY

I will never forget a middle-age couple who stopped by our church one afternoon. They were living in an old car, badly in need of repair. They needed financial help, and my heart was touched by their despair. After having repaired their car and given them food and money, I sent them on their way, hoping our benevolence would lift them from their misfortune and give them the hope they needed to rebuild their lives.

One year later, this couple came by our church again, still in the same car, and still in need of financial help. Apparently, they had stopped at many churches along the way and forgotten they had visited us before. The first time I met this couple my heart went out to them because I couldn't imagine myself living in their situation. This time, when I recognized them and understood their condition, I was less sympathetic. It was now

---

Do not accept the devil's lie that you cannot change and that your home cannot be happy.

---

obvious that this couple's problem was not with their immediate need, but rather their long-term need of finding a job and learning to become responsible. After a brief discussion, I soon realized they were unwilling to accept my advice. This couple needed a change of heart; an internal correction that would lead them to accept responsibility for themselves and no longer require help from others. Every family needs to have the right heart attitude about the home. If your heart is not right, you must change your attitude. Do not accept the devil's lie that you cannot change and that your home cannot be happy. *The real issue is not a matter of can or cannot, but of will or will not!*

> "I can do all things through Christ which strengtheneth me" (Philippians 4:13).

Troubled families often act shortsightedly by using a band-aid to heal a heart problem. Seeking counsel is vain if the counsel is not followed. Getting counseling, reading how-to books, or even getting a new spouse or new family is not enough. We need a burning desire to make our home a godly home. Except for your commitment to God, your home should be your first priority.

Recently my parents celebrated their fiftieth wedding anniversary. Someone trying to make a joke stated, "Well it looks like this one might last." My mother, in no so subtle manner, replied, "That was settled long ago." A happy home is an issue of the heart.

Envision a Happy Home

Can you envision a godly home? If not, perhaps your understanding of a happy home is deficient. We tend to use our own standard in measuring our home's success, but we should measure our homes by the standard of God's Word. Would you be surprised to know there are homes filled with joy and peace rather than arguing and fighting? We are all limited by our own frame of reference, making it difficult to envision any other setting for our family. Our parents' mistakes—and our own—can be passed on to succeeding generations.

We can change our paradigm through applying biblical principles learned through listening to sermons, reading good books, attending conferences on the family, and seeking godly counsel. Every person's knowledge of the home comes primarily from experiences passed on through their parents, thus we must broaden our scope to include positive sources. Even though couples determine they will never make their parents' mistakes, too often they repeat the same mistakes again and again. That chain can be broken by the power of God's Word.

I am surprised that few married couples take advantage of the storehouse of good marriage and family information available to them. Understandably, couples who are overwhelmed by problems often are too embarrassed to ask for help. They do not realize that, by making their family a priority, their home could be a haven, safe from the world's conflicts and problems; a place they would be happy to call *home*. Help is available for those sincerely seeking it.

I recall a story my basketball coach told us long ago. Before he was a Christian, he became quite angry with his wife. To spare her, he took out his frustration by punching a hole

---

Even though couples determine they will never make their parents' mistakes, too often they repeat the same mistakes again and again.

---

in the kitchen wall. His sweet wife placed a beautiful plaque over the offending hole. The phrase "God bless this Home" graced that wall for a long while. It was a wonderful message, but meaningless without the proper heart. Many families have tried to mask the failure of their homes with the façade of religious piety, but beneath the surface is a deep hole of emptiness.

Making money and pursuing hobbies are poor substitutes for life priorities. I have never conducted a funeral where it was said of the deceased that he wished he had spent more time at work or more time becoming a success. However, I have heard of many who, facing the end of their life, regretted that they had not invested more time into their home. A happy home is a treasure beyond compare. Blessed are the man and the woman who have learned to build their home upon God's Word. Are you covering up the reality of a failing home? Do you need help to change your paradigm? Determine in your heart to build your home on God's Word.

God's Plan For The Home

Chapter Two

Precious Memories

My parents understood the structure of the home. My father was a hard worker, in spite of his small stature, and I never doubted that he was the head of our home. I feared and respected my father like no other man on the earth. I never doubted my mother's love for me either. My parents were deeply committed to our home. I cannot recall my parents ever disagreeing on how we were to be raised. Whenever I sought permission for something, they always agreed on the answer.

My wife and I were able to glean many good qualities from our families as we began our new home. In addition to the heritage provided by our families, we enrolled in a class titled "Courtship and Marriage," while still in college. Our college training provided seminars and preaching on the home as well as a wonderful library containing many helpful books and articles about the home. We were in the perfect environment to learn about the home.

Our first year of marriage was busy with college, work, and ministry, but the memory of those early years still fills my mind and heart with joy when I realize that we were armed with the authority of God's Word. I praise the Lord for His guidance in our lives.

Marriage principles that worked in the past still work today. Though the Bible truths concerning marriage were written hundreds of years ago human nature has remained unchanged. Old does not necessarily mean bad. Simple common sense principles are illustrated by the following comments:

COUNTRY SENSE

- The biggest troublemaker you'll probably ever have to deal with watches you shave your face in the mirror every morning.
- Your fences need to be horse-high, pig-tight, and bull-strong.
- Life is simpler if you plow around the stump.
- When you wallow with pigs, expect to get dirty.
- Bumblebees are considerably faster than a John Deere tractor.
- The best sermons are lived, not preached.
- Live a good, honorable life. Then when you get older and think back, you'll enjoy it a second time.
- Live simply. Love generously. Care deeply. Speak kindly. Leave the rest to God.

A Godly Heritage

As I look back on my childhood I believe I had a sense of security from knowing that there were certain decisions I did not have to make. My father and mother knew I was not yet ready to make them. I greatly admired my father and I wanted very much to be like him. He taught me to love my mother, though that was easy to do. He directed my life the way he felt it should go. I remember one time I wanted to run away from home, but my father would not let me, and I could not bring myself to disobey Dad. I never thought of my dad as my best friend; I always thought of him as my father. I found many good friends, but no one else could become my father. I have always greatly respected my parents, and my wife can say the same of her parents as well. Our parents were deeply committed to their homes.

In addition to the wonderful pattern we learned from our parents, my wife and I have tried to learn and glean from every available resource to enhance our home. We have dozens of books on the home, and we have attended many seminars and listened to many lectures. We have both carefully studied the Bible's teachings on parenting and the roles of husbands and wives. We have worked hard to follow God's plan for the home, and now we rejoice to watch our children learning to follow the same pattern in their homes. Following Biblical principles has been the key to our marriage and the key to rearing our children. Anyone willing to follow the Bible's clear teaching will discover practical solutions that are at once both old-fashioned and contemporary. What a blessing to know we have the authority of the Word of God, which never changes!

GOD DESIGNED THE HOME

The most foundational truth about the home is that it was God's idea. God's plan for the home is revealed in the first three chapters of Genesis. Here we see that God created man and woman in His own image. The book of Colossians explains that our resemblance to God is not physical. Rather, unlike the animals, man has knowledge and morality, and man is a religious creature. The first man, Adam, was the smartest and holiest man ever to live on the earth. But, when he sinned that quickly changed and God's image in man was tarnished.

Just as God sacrificed innocent animals to provide a covering for man's nakedness (Genesis 3:21), so today God has provided His own Son as an innocent sacrifice to pay for our sins and provide for us a cloak of righteousness. Man has failed through his sin, but where sin abounded, grace did much more abound (Romans 5:20). Through God's grace we can be restored to God when we put our trust in His Son's sacrifice. A Christian home is impossible apart from a man and a woman being saved through faith in the shed blood of Christ. A godly home can be established only where both spouses know Christ as their Savior and heed the Holy Spirit's leading in their lives.

- "Wherefore, as by one man sin entered into the world, and death by sin; and so death passed upon all men, for that all have sinned" (Romans 5:12).
- "For as by one man's disobedience many were made sinners, so by the obedience of one shall many be made righteous" (Romans 5:19).

Reflecting upon the completion of creation, God states that it was *good*, which includes the home. Before civil government and before the Church existed, God instituted the home. God blessed the man and the woman, and God said that all His creation was good. We must realize that God's plan cannot be improved. Problems in the home are never the result of God devising a poor plan but of man's failure at instituting what God has ordained. Every couple that carefully builds their home on God's divine plan will have a successful home!

EVALUATING YOUR HOME

An honest evaluation of your home can be a difficult task. How can you determine the quality of your home? Our conclusions are based upon our knowledge, and if our knowledge is inadequate, then we will have difficulty properly evaluating our success. Often the only knowledge a couple may have is their observations of their own parents. Some parents, husbands, or wives may seek advice from friends or co-workers whose Bible knowledge is limited or lacking. Godly parents or a godly pastor and his wife can be wonderful resources. A godly couple from church can also be a great inspiration. However we choose to evaluate our home, the method must be Biblical. Ultimately, success or failure must be determined by God's Word.

Counseling hundreds of people has given me great insight concerning home life. When counseling, I often ask, "How would you describe your home life?" Or, "How would you describe the home in which you were reared?" I'm amazed how frequently people try to paint a rosy picture of their home, when in fact their home is falling apart. They find it difficult to admit they have failed, and often they respond, "Oh, we have our difficulties, just like everyone else." Or they say, "My parents had their troubles, but they were no different than everyone else's." As far as these couples know, screaming and arguing is normal in every home. They have nothing to compare their own home to. But, if they could secretly observe the actions of a healthy Christian family, they would soon realize that their home is not normal by God's standard. Let me reiterate that no family is perfect, and all families need to improve their homes and make them stronger. But, some families fail to realize that their homes are in trouble.

Many a well-meaning parent has defended a child's behavior by claiming, "All children have to go through a time of rebellion and sow their wild oats." This is not true, and is not Biblical! The Bible states, "Train up a child in the way he should go: and when he is old, he will not depart from it" (Proverbs 22:6). This verse specifies that a child properly trained will never leave his training while he is growing or after he leaves the home. I can give many examples of godly Christian homes where all children were obedient and never rebelled. The misguided notion that all children rebel, adds to the confusion and ignores the mistakes that are already being made.

Often when a couple comes to me for counsel, I find it difficult to identify their specific problems because they're on their best behavior at church or sitting in the preacher's office. After years of counseling experience, I have become more successful at understanding the problems in a counseling session, but it would be a hundred times easier if I could secretly observe the home in action for a day. If parents will learn to be humble and forthcoming, they will greatly enhance the process of evaluating their home properly so that they can begin to make the necessary changes.

A Christian couple should have a time for daily Bible reading and prayer.

Problems in the home always begin at the beginning. When the excitement of the new marriage wears off, the reality of what each spouse believes is manifested. Starting out on the right path is extremely important for every couple. A Christian couple should have a time for daily Bible reading and prayer. If this is not accomplished as a young couple, it is unlikely that it will be added later. Praying together provides an opportunity for couples to open their heart to the Lord and each other so that their marital relationship is enhanced. Reading the Scripture together gives you a common spiritual bond that refines your relationship.

In the process of counseling young couples for marriage, I recently learned of a new trend. Worldly individuals are questioning prospective couples about the sanity of marriage: "Why get married? You'll be sorry. Just wait and you'll see." Having heard that advice, would-be couples ask me, "Is it that bad to be married?" My reply to them is clear. The most wonderful experience in this life is to have a Christian home. The Bible clearly states that "marriage is honorable" and "he that findeth a wife findeth a good thing." God created the home and said, "It was good." God made no mistake in designing the institutions of and patterns for marriage and the home.

Marriage is More Than a Commitment to Cohabitate

Many believe that every young couple should just live together and not face the responsibility of marriage, but God calls this fornication. God's plan involves obedience to the laws of the magistrates (Romans 13). Although civil law does not require marriage to cohabitate, full recognition of marriage by the law is necessary to honor God. Without submission to the law of the land, marriage is denigrated to the whims of an individual's emotional desire. The Bible says marriage creates one from two. Two becoming one means the man must accept the responsibilities of being the husband and leader of the home. In addition, it means he will forsake all others and cleave to his wife. Any couple who considers their commitment to be sincere should acquire a license and follow the marriage laws of the land, resulting in legal recognition of their marriage. To do less is a heinous error.

Before Adam and Eve had children, God explained that a man was to leave father and mother and cleave to his wife. In God's omniscience He prepared Adam and Eve to prepare their children for the future. The simplest way to describe marriage is one man and one woman *for life*. God's plan was not for two men or two women, nor did God structure the home to consist of several men or combinations of men and women. So what constitutes a marriage? Is love enough to constitute marriage? No! God created a man and a woman to make a marriage. God gave the woman to the man. Anything else is a perversion of God's perfect plan. There are four requirements for people to be married.

1. A commitment to each other to be husband and wife (1 Corinthians 7:2)
2. A completion of government's requirements for marriage (Titus 3:1)
3. A physical consummation of the marriage (Ephesians 5:31)
4. "And said, For this cause shall a man leave father and mother, and shall cleave to his wife: and they twain shall be one flesh? Wherefore they are no more twain, but one flesh. What therefore God hath joined together, let not man put asunder." (Matthew 19:5-6)

The woman was a fulfillment of everything the man needed in order to be happy and to bring glory to God.

God could have created the home in any fashion He chose, yet He created the prototype home in a very specific way: He created man from the dust of the ground, and gave him a purpose in tending the garden and bringing glory to his Creator. Adam named all the animals of the earth, and yet he was unfulfilled and alone. God recognized man's need and so He brought the woman to the man. Eve was to be a helpmeet (a perfectly matched partner) fitting for Adam. The woman was a fulfillment of everything the man needed in order to be happy and to bring glory to God. This first home was the happiest home that ever existed. God made male and female, and declared it to be good. Before sin, Adam and Eve enjoyed all God had intended for them. But they disobeyed, and sin separated them from God. Now their home needed restoration. God judged them, but He also showed them grace. For every failure, God's grace is within reach to bring us back to Him.

The Failure and Restoration of the First Home

Every home has been influenced by the first couple's fall in the garden. Because of humanity's sinful condition, structure within the home has become necessary. A clear structure of authority and purpose was given to help reconcile and protect the first home. God gave each person a specific role to fulfill. You may try to ignore God's structure for the home, but you cannot change it.

God's plan included the children that were yet to be born. God told the couple to be fruitful and multiply. In other words, God intended one man for one woman for life—a union that would produce children who would likewise follow God's plan. This plan would glorify Him and give humans regency rule over the earth.

Of course, every Christian knows the account of man's failure. Sin brought death (spiritual and physical) to the first couple and all their progeny. Mankind failed at God's perfect plan; however, through God's grace, man was given a new opportunity to please Him. That opportunity meant man had to respond to God's grace and turn to Him. Since the beginning of creation mankind has repeated this same story. God has a plan; man fails in following the plan; then God gives man

Remember that God has a plan for every home, and that plan begins with salvation.

the opportunity to respond to His grace. As man learns to respond to God's grace, man is able to restore the home and build it according to Biblical principles.

Remember that God has a plan for every home, and that plan begins with salvation. To have a Christian home the members need to be restored to God by admitting they are lost sinners and that Christ died for their sin. All who recognize their lost condition, turn to Christ for salvation, and call on Him by repentance and faith will be born again into God's family. Without salvation, it is impossible to have a Christian home. If every member of the family receives Christ as his Savior, then the family will have a foundation to build a Christian home. In Matthew 7 Jesus equates a life apart from His salvation with building a house on sand. That comparison also applies to building a home. The winds and rain will come and destroy that house and great will be its fall. The wise man will build his home upon a rock, and that rock is Christ.

THE BIBLICAL STRUCTURE OF THE HOME

As a child I always felt secure by my parent's relationship. I knew they were happily married and there was never a hint that would change.

Notice, the Bible is clear that marriage is between one man and one woman, not two men or two women or multiple partners. God did not intend for people to marry, divorce, and marry again. It is His intent that marriage be between one man and one woman for life.

> "Wherefore they are no more twain, but one flesh. What therefore God hath joined together, let not man put asunder. They say unto him, Why did Moses then command to give a writing of divorcement, and to put her away? He saith unto them, Moses because of the hardness of your hearts suffered you to put away your wives: but from the beginning it was not so" (Matthew 19:6-8).

To build on Christ's foundation is to recognize that God has a structure in the home and every person has a role to fulfill. God's design can never be improved. It is always up to date and right for every culture. The structure of authority is one of the most difficult teachings to understand. Many seem to think God did not really consider their situation because, if He had, He would not have said what He did. Some have believed Satan's lie that if they follow Scripture their lives will be boring and pitiful.

The same situation existed in the Garden of Eden. The devil said, "Yea hath God said." The devil also tried to help Eve justify her sin by rationalizing, "God doth know that you shall be as gods." Many today are falling prey to Satan's lies. Somehow they think they will be unhappy and miss all the fun if they follow God's plan. So instead, they follow their selfish desires, which lead to sorrow and pain. The grass always appears greener on the other side, *until you get to the other side*. Believe me; many *on the other side* envy those who are in God's will. Every home that follows God's authority will be happy and contented. The following diagram clearly shows the simple structure of the home, with God clearly at the head. If the Lord is always first, then everything else can be in its proper order. If God is not in first place, then everything else is in chaos.

GOD

⌄

JESUS CHRIST

⌄

FATHER

⌄

MOTHER

⌄

CHILDREN

THE ROLE OF A HUSBAND

First let us consider the role of the husband and father in the Christian home. What is the role for every husband and father? The Bible teaches us that the man is to be the head of the wife. The head represents knowledge and leadership. The man must make decisions that will benefit his home, and not just his personal and selfish desires. First Corinthians 11:3 says, "But I would have you know, that the head of every man is Christ; and the head of the woman is the man; and the head of Christ is God." Every man has the responsibility to seek God's will for his home. The real head of the home is God, but God uses the structure of authority to carry out His plan. Every man must submit himself to God, but also to his wife by being willing to take the role of being the spiritual head (Ephesians 5:2). A man can choose to give his wife her every whim, or he can rule her with a rod of iron. Neither extreme is Biblical. The only Biblical method is for a husband to lead his wife with love and self–sacrifice (Ephesians 5:28-32).

The husband is the head of the home only as he follows Christ. The husband must be a spiritual man if he is to fulfill the Scriptural teaching on being the head of his home. "For the husband is the head of the wife, even as Christ is the head of the church: and he is the Saviour of the body" (Ephesians 5:23). Christ gave himself to save the Church; as He provided and preserved that Church, so ought the husband to manifest a similar attitude to make his wife happy and to save her from want, affliction, and pain. He ought to regard himself as her protector; to anticipate and provide for her needs and to comfort her in trial, even as Christ does for the Church. What a beautiful illustration: A husband should manifest in his relationship to his wife the same care Christ has shown for his "bride," the Church! The extent of a man's love for his wife should be to love her as he loves himself. So ought men to love their wives as their own bodies. "He that loveth his wife loveth himself" (Ephesians 5:28). Every man does a good job of loving himself, but we must love our wife to that same extent. Love is a noun, but it is also a verb. Particularly in marriage, love is the action of giving. Love is giving of oneself to another.

The Bible has a principle some have named the "leave and cleave principle." Upon marriage, a man must leave his parents and cleave to his wife. This means that a man must leave physically. He must move out of his parents' home. If he can't afford to pay his own rent, then he should wait to get married. He must not depend on his parents for his basic needs. However difficult it may be, upon marriage, every man must cut the apron strings and make it on his own. A man and woman must also leave their childhood homes emotionally. Your spouse should be the joy of your life. Every wife's

---

Particularly in marriage, love is the action of giving.

---

provider and prince charming should be her husband. Also, a man is to cleave ("to be faithful: *cleave to one's principles*") to his wife and, forsaking all others, learn to depend on her for his needs. Couples must learn to depend on each other. If you do not learn to cleave to your spouse, someone else may come along who will. "For this cause shall a man leave his father and mother, and shall be joined unto his wife, and they two shall be one flesh" (Ephesians 5:31). Every marriage involves emotional, physical, and spiritual needs. Because the wife's position is under the authority of the husband, the man must recognize her position of trust to him. He must take great care to ensure that all of her needs are met.

- "Likewise, ye husbands, dwell with them according to knowledge, giving honour unto the wife, as unto the weaker vessel, and as being heirs together of the grace of life; that your prayers be not hindered" (1 Peter 3:7).

- "Let the husband render unto the wife due benevolence: and likewise also the wife unto the husband. The wife hath not power of her own body, but the husband: and likewise also the husband hath not power of his own body, but the wife. Defraud ye not one the other, except it be with consent for a time, that ye may give yourselves to fasting and prayer; and come together again, that Satan tempt you not for your incontinency" (1 Corinthians 7:3-5).
- "Let thy fountain be blessed: and rejoice with the wife of thy youth" (Proverbs 5:18).

Mothers offer something to small children that men can't easily imitate; conversely men offer certain dynamics to their children that are uniquely suited to their role. Sometimes I would stop by home and find my wife was overwhelmed by her duties with our children. Often I would pile the kids in the car and take them with me. In fact, every opportunity I had I would take one or more of the children with me while I completed my errands. These brief encounters offered an opportunity to bond and develop special relationships with each child. Every father has a responsibility to ensure that his children have been given proper direction and provision. A father can have a negative impact on his children or a positive impact upon them. Therefore it is important for every father to learn to be an encouragement for his children to live for God.

- "Fathers, provoke not your children to anger, lest they be discouraged" (Colossians 3:21).
- "And, ye fathers, provoke not your children to wrath: but bring them up in the nurture and admonition of the Lord" (Ephesians 6:4).

The father must chasten his children when necessary. Also the father must teach, warn, and direct his children. Every father must earn his family's respect. To summarize, a husband's role is to be the prophet, priest, and king of his home.

There is no better sermon than a father who lives in the home what he says in church.

As a priest, the father is to be the spiritual leader of his wife and children. Husbands and fathers should lead their family to love and serve the Lord. Dad should lead the way to faithful church attendance and Christian service as well as family devotions and family prayer. There is no better sermon than a father who lives in the home what he says in church.

In addition, a father must protect his family from thieves, pedophiles, worldly influences, and danger. Not only must he protect his family from external dangers, but from internal as well. He must recognize the dangers (such as discouragement, jealousy, gossip, envy, etc.) his wife may face and protect her from them. Every father knows his daughter will eventually become a teen and probably someday be married. A father must protect his daughter from the pitfalls awaiting her. Every young girl wants to be noticed and appreciated; if a father doesn't meet these needs the wrong people can influence her future.

Finally, every man must provide for his family. Every man is born with a basic instinct that prods him to provide food, shelter and clothing for his family. This drive is strong and must be kept in perspective. But if any provide not for his own, and specially for those of his own house, he hath denied the faith, and is worse than an infidel. (1 Timothy 5:8) However, providing for his family's material needs is only part of his responsibility, he must also provide security, confidence and a sense of well being. The example set by every father will ultimately reflect to his children their perception of a heavenly Father, thus his role is vital to their understanding of God.

I recall my youngest daughter coming home from school one day upset, because other girls were teasing her concerning her position on the basketball team. She was the youngest player on the team and a bit of jealousy had developed among the girls. After listening to her plight I responded to her, "Sarah you are a very good player and they are jealous of your ability." I admonished her to continue her humble spirit and play to the best of her ability. After I explained she had done nothing wrong and that she could maintain a positive testimony to her team mates she was satisfied and went on her way. She simply needed approval and encouragement from her dad.

The Role of a Wife

"Unto the woman he said, I will greatly multiply thy sorrow and thy conception; in sorrow thou shalt bring forth children;

and thy desire shall be to thy husband, and he shall rule over thee. God created woman to be a help to the man" (Genesis 3:16). Eve possessed everything Adam needed for his life to be fulfilled, but sin changed their relationship. Because of sin, an order of authority was needed. Every wife must understand submission to her husband. Anyone who rejects submission to human authority is rejecting God's authority. God's plan must be seen as superior. Through obedience to God's plan comes great success and happiness.

- "Wives, submit yourselves unto your own husbands, as unto the Lord" (Ephesians 5:22).
- "Therefore as the church is subject unto Christ, so let the wives be to their own husbands in every thing" (Ephesians 5:24).
- "Likewise, ye wives, be in subjection to your own husbands; that, if any obey not the word, they also may without the word be won by the conversation of the wives; While they behold your chaste conversation coupled with fear. Whose adorning let it not be that outward adorning of plaiting the hair, and of wearing of gold, or of putting on of apparel; But let it be the hidden man of the heart, in that which is not corruptible, even the ornament of a meek and quiet spirit, which is in the sight of God of great price. For after this manner in the old time the holy women also, who trusted in God, adorned themselves, being in subjection unto their own husbands" (1 Peter 3:1-5).
- "In like manner also, that women adorn themselves in modest apparel, with shamefacedness and sobriety;

not with broided hair, or gold, or pearls, or costly array; But (which becometh women professing godliness) with good works" (1 Timothy 2:9-10).

- "That they may teach the young women to be sober, to love their husbands, to love their children, To be discreet, chaste, keepers at home, good, obedient to their own husbands, that the word of God be not blasphemed" (Titus 2:4-5).
- "I will therefore that the younger women marry, bear children, guide the house, give none occasion to the adversary to speak reproachfully" (1 Timothy 5:14).

The scriptural teaching on this subject is abundant. Why then is it so difficult for wives to grasp this wonderful truth? The reason is simple. Only a spiritual mind can grasp spiritual truth. Those who use human reason to evaluate this teaching on submission likely will conclude it is "unfair." The spiritual mind however will trust God and His word. God then proves Himself through the woman's submission and faith.

The woman who submits to God by submitting to her husband finds great peace and blessing.

A similar principle is found in other Biblical truths. To really live, you must first die. The pathway to prominence is through humility. Give and you will receive. The same thing is true of submission. The woman who will not submit will never receive peace and fulfillment. The woman who submits to God by submitting to her husband finds great peace and blessing. Someone has said, "The weaker sex is actually the stronger sex because of the weakness of the stronger sex for the weaker sex." In other words, when a woman is submissive to her husband, he will do anything for her. When she tries to fight with him and nag to get her way, he has no positive incentive to help her. In fact, she has demeaned the man's position and relegated him to a position of submission. A man like that may endure the relationship, but will have a noodle for a backbone. I do not think any wife really wants a husband with no backbone.

The Role of Children

- "Children, obey your parents in the Lord: for this is right. Honour thy father and mother; (which is the first commandment with promise;) That it may be well with thee, and thou mayest live long on the earth" (Ephesians 6:1-3).
- "Young men likewise exhort to be sober minded. In all things shewing thyself a pattern of good works: in doctrine shewing uncorruptness, gravity, sincerity, Sound speech, that cannot be condemned; that he that is of the contrary part may be ashamed, having no evil thing to say of you" (Titus 2:6-8).
- "Let no man despise thy youth; but be thou an example of the believers, in word, in conversation, in charity, in spirit, in faith, in purity" (1 Timothy 4:12).
- "Flee also youthful lusts: but follow righteousness, faith, charity, peace, with them that call on the Lord

out of a pure heart" (2 Timothy 2:22)

- "Do all things without murmurings and disputings" (Philippians 2:14).
- "Children, obey your parents in all things: for this is well pleasing unto the Lord" (Colossians 3:20).

Children also have a role to play. Their role does not involve parenting or leading the home in any way. Children's role is to obey their parents. If children learn this valuable lesson, they will be successful in life. Ephesians 6:1-3 refers to Exodus 20:12. The fifth commandment is the first commandment accompanied by a promise. The promise is that if a child honors his parents, his life will be good and long. Why? Obedience to authority affects all aspects of one's future relationships. If a child can learn honor in the home, he will have it all through life. A child whose parents allow him to run the home will suffer dire consequences later in life. It is the parents' responsibility to teach their children to respect them and their authority. This teaching must be accomplished through word and deed. Respect must be modeled, earned, and expected. There can be no greater failure than failing to teach children this wonderful truth that obedience is God's plan.

My wife knew a family that adopted two children. The parents were not wealthy, but they constantly sacrificed to give their children everything they desired. Nothing was withheld from the children. When the children grew to adulthood, they both rebelled against their parents. The girl ran away from home, and the boy was constantly in trouble with the law. Both children disgraced and saddened these parents.

The parents gave their children everything except what they needed: respect for and obedience to authority. Some parents falsely assume that correcting a child will lead him to reject his parents. The exact opposite is true. "The rod and reproof give wisdom: but a child left to himself bringeth his mother to shame" (Proverbs 29:15). A parent must give a child what he needs, not what he wants.

The most valuable asset you can give your children is godly character.

A son asked his wealthy father, "Are we wealthy?" The dad replied, "No, your mother and I are wealthy, but you have nothing." The one thing the child possessed was a parent determined to teach his son to become responsible. In that sense, the son was very wealthy. The most valuable asset you can give your children is godly character. If they have character, they can accomplish anything God leads them to do.

The Greatest Thing

Chapter Three

Precious Memories

As a young man I enjoyed success, at least as I perceived it. I was athletic, admired by my peers, and the president of my class, but in one area of my life I had no common sense: I didn't know how to find a good wife. Though not a Christian, finding the right mate for life was vitally important to me. I prayed nightly for God to provide me with the proper mate. I looked forward to that day with great anticipation; however I was on a crash course to make a wrong decision.

My life suddenly changed when I left a large state college to attend a small Christian College. I went to the smaller Christian College for the wrong motive: to play basketball. I had never heard of a Christian College, I knew only one thing about this school: it had a basketball team. Three months after I arrived there I became a born-again Christian, and my life changed dramatically and immediately. One year after becoming a Christian God led me to a wonderful Christian girl who I married six months later.

I'll always remember the day we were sitting on the sofa in her parents' home as we discussed our future. I suddenly became overwhelmed with emotion and the tears began to flow. Janet quickly inquired what was wrong because she had never before seen me cry. I told her I was overwhelmed with joy that God would provide me with a good Christian wife, and by the prospect of Christian home. I know I came close to making a big mistake, but by His grace God had spared me. I am so thankful that God gave me a wonderful helpmeet to serve together with me in the ministry and to bear and rear our children. A Christian marriage is the greatest thing in the world!

Marriage Is the Greatest Thing

"And now abideth faith, hope, charity, these three; but the greatest of these is charity" (1 Corinthians 13:13). The word charity is translated form the Greek word agape. Agape is a sacrificial and giving love. A giving love is the kind of love exemplified by God in giving His only begotten Son on the cross of Calvary. Marriage affords daily opportunities to express agape love. Henry Drummond's famous sermon, "The Greatest Thing in the World" is a classic exposition on First Corinthians chapter thirteen where he extols the virtues of agape love. This First Corinthians passage indicates that love is the greatest virtue. Marriage that is built on a giving love is the greatest thing in the world; there is nothing else in this world like it.

- "Marriage is honourable in all, and the bed undefiled: but whoremongers and adulterers God will judge" (Hebrews 13:4).
- "Whoso findeth a wife findeth a good thing, and obtaineth favour of the LORD" (Proverbs 18:22).
- "There be three things which are too wonderful for me, yea, four which I know not: The way of an eagle in the air; the way of a serpent upon a rock; the way of a ship in the midst of the sea; and the way of a man with a maid" (Proverbs 30:18-19).

A godly Christian home reflects a wonderful imitation of God himself.

God wants us to know that marriage is meant to be a wonderful experience. A godly Christian home reflects a wonderful imitation of God himself. The world can see Christ through your relationship. Consequently, the greatest evidence of Christ to the world will be your love. First Corinthians chapter thirteen is called the love chapter of the Bible. Verse thirteen says, "Now abideth faith hope and charity, but the greatest of these is charity." Marriage is intended to bring glory to God and joy to His people. Both of these things will be true in a godly marriage.

Love is the most valuable of all the virtues mentioned, but it is crucial that we understand the real meaning of love. The world has so perverted the word that it has come to seen almost as the opposite of its real meaning. Biblical love gives with a sacrificial spirit. Biblical love does not seek its own benefit and always puts others first. The world has led us to believe that love is something you get not something you give. The one recognizable characteristic of the early Church was that Christians were known by their love. There is no substitute for love in the home. Love begins with the husband and wife and then spreads to the children. Children should literally come into a world that is a sea of love. Love is displayed through affection, giving gifts, serving others, and putting others before you.

My role as pastor has allowed me to see the best and also the worst in people. One statement I hear often is, "I don't love him (or her) anymore." I want to shout, "Then learn to obey God: Love him!" Love is a command. Someone reading this will respond, "You can't expect me to love her after what she did to me." The misunderstanding is really quite simple.

When couples learn the biblical way to live the emotion of love always follows.

People are saying, "The emotion is gone from my marriage." But, I'm saying, "The reason the emotion is gone is because you are not choosing to love each other." I hear an admission of guilt when someone says, "I don't love him anymore." Marriage has its challenges and difficulties. When those difficulties come, spouses need to realize love is especially important. The emotion of a newly married couple will last only a few months. When reality hits the real marriage begins to be built or destroyed.

American's idea of marriage has become twisted and inaccurate. We all need to understand the true meaning of love. When we understand and experience true Biblical love, marriage will have more emotion than ever anticipated. How can there be a warm fuzzy feeling for your spouse when you live selfishly? Anyone who lives in a home where there is yelling, fighting, jealousy, and infidelity will always have difficulty experiencing positive emotion and feelings. But, when true love is employed there will be sacrificing, forgiveness, kindness, and affection. When couples learn the biblical way to live the emotion of love always follows. Ask yourself this question: How much do I put into my marriage? What you put into your marriage will determine what you get out of it.

THE LOVE CHAPTER OF THE BIBLE

> "Charity suffereth long, and is kind; charity envieth not; charity vaunteth not itself, is not puffed up, Doth not behave itself unseemly, seeketh not her own, is not easily provoked, thinketh no evil; Rejoiceth not in iniquity, but rejoiceth in the truth; Beareth all things, believeth all things, hopeth all things, endureth all things. Charity never faileth: but whether there be prophecies, they shall fail; whether there be tongues, they shall cease; whether there be knowledge, it shall vanish away" (1 Corinthians 13:4-8).

This passage was the first chapter my wife and I memorized together. We enjoyed memorizing this passage because it had so much meaning to us and we never wanted our marriage to become stale. Everyone who reads and employs the teaching of this chapter will most certainly reap the benefits of it as well.

This amazing passage describes the biblical manifestation of genuine love, which is given rather than received. Agape describes affection as a sacrificial action for the benefit of another. Selfishness wants, but true love gives. Selfishness destroys a marriage, while giving builds it. Selfishness demands, while love understands. When two people argue, complain, and seek to hurt one another their home is in trouble.

Marriage is not fifty-fifty, it is one hundred-nothing. We each belong completely to the other. Husbands are to love their wives as Christ loved the Church and gave himself for it.

- "Husbands, love your wives, even as Christ also loved the church, and gave himself for it" (Ephesians 5:25).
- "Let the husband render unto the wife due benevolence: and likewise also the wife unto the husband. The wife hath not power of her own body, but the husband: and likewise also the husband hath not power of his own body, but the wife" (1 Corinthians 7:3-4).

It is difficult to comprehend, but regardless of your spouse's actions you should still give yourself unreservedly to them. True love is unconditional, just like God's love for us.

The Right Kind of Love

Several Greek words are used to describe love. The word love is often used to mean lust; desiring what is forbidden, or concupiscence. Concupiscence describes an evil desire that grows and becomes more sinful over time. That is how sin always works. It begins small and then grows out of control. In other words, one sin leads to another, then another and so on. Our word erotic comes from the Greek word eros. It refers to a sensual love that is self-serving and self-gratifying. Hollywood glamorizes this type of "love" as something to be desired, yet in the end it leads to destruction. Through fashion and culture young men and women are encouraged to be

---

Girls must be taught to be chaste and godly in the way they dress and behave.

---

sexy. Inappropriate dress for Christian women is alluded to in Proverbs 7:10, while a godly example of attire is given in 1 Peter 3:2-4. A woman's modest fashion exemplifies her godly character and strengthens her countenance and radiance; conversely worldly fashions bring attention to a woman's physical appearance which will only cheapen her testimony.

Many young people today have accepted this eros lifestyle as normal. The latest fashions tend to be too short, too low, too thin, or too tight. Parents must recognize the potential problems and guide their children to be a godly example. Girls must be taught to be chaste and godly in the way they dress and behave. "That they may teach the young women to be sober, to love their husbands, to love their children, To be discreet, chaste, keepers at home, good, obedient to their own husbands, that the word of God be not blasphemed" (Titus 2:4-5).

Prior to my boys reaching their teen years I sat down with them individually to discuss marriage from a Biblical viewpoint. After speaking with my second son, who was twelve at the time, I asked him if he had heard anything about this before our conversation. I was pleased to hear him reply this was the first anyone had spoken to him. At that time I felt gratified to know he had heard a Biblical perspective before the world could give him a perverted view of this holy institution called marriage.

Another Greek word, phileo, suggests a friendship or a companionship. Being friends is a commendable thing. The Lord asked Peter, "Do you love me?" Jesus was asking, "Do you love me with an agape type of love?" Peter could only respond with, "Lord you know that I love you," (phileo) as a friend. Peter had pledged to the Lord that he would never deny Him, but after Peter's denial he found it difficult to claim to have the deepest level of love. Though friendships are to be encouraged, there is still a higher level of love.

Love is a choice that grows incrementally.

The Greek word agape can only mean self-sacrificing love, the kind of love illustrated in John 3:16: "For God so loved the world that he gave his only begotten Son, that whosoever believeth in him should not perish, but have everlasting life." The highest level of love was clearly expressed by God in giving of His only begotten Son, Jesus Christ. The pattern for every home is to exhibit self-sacrificing love. This is love that expects nothing in return.

Love is a choice that grows incrementally. What if the love is gone? Should you pretend? Love is based on God's love to us, and out of God's love we show love by our actions. Marriage is made up of a lot of little things. Surprisingly, many couples couldn't tell you the root of their marriage problems. Their relationship has become confusing and full of tension. When they stopped doing the little things, they stopped building the marriage. If you are kind and show your love through little things, then eventually the love (noun) returns. Don't expect romance to mystically appear until you give yourself unreservedly to your mate.

BUILDING YOUR MARRIAGE

Matthew 7:24-27 reveals that the foundation of a house must be strong if it is to stand the torrents of a storm: "And the rain descended, and the floods came, and the winds blew, and beat upon that house; and it fell: and great was the fall of it." Homes don't build themselves. When building your home you must begin with the foundation. If the foundation is not secure, you face the possibility of erecting a beautiful structure that will fall in the face of a storm. The only sure foundation is Christ. When Christ is the head, right choices will be made that honor Him.

Building requires effort and attention. Building a home requires emotional, spiritual, physical, and time investments. True emotion springs from the heart, the center-most part of our being. The ability to share our innermost feelings and thoughts can be difficult. However, when we become transparent we find a new freedom within our marriage that produces an inner peace. There are many tangible ways to express love for one another. A telephone call form work just to say, "I love you," or preparing a special treat of cookies for your husband when he returns home from work are good expressions of love. Encouraging words of thankfulness can be expressed verbally and in special notes. Pleasant surprises such as flowers or a dinner date can mean a lot. Love can grow when it is expressed openly and freely.

How can a young couple be in love in the beginning of their relationship and later lose the joy of the marriage? A marriage that is constantly being built will not allow this to happen. However, when things are allowed to build up without resolve they can soon explode and begin a downward spiral. The Bible teaches us to "Be ye angry, and sin not: let not the sun go down upon your wrath: Neither give place to the devil" (Ephesians 4:26, 27). When a conflict arises it must be dealt with the same day. To retire to bed with anger is a formula for disaster. If an issue is resolved the same day it occurs it will not become unmanageable. There may be some late nights that require discussion, confession, and forgiveness, but those issues will not hamper continued fidelity. Your marriage is the most important relationship you have on this earth. At the end of your life I am certain you will find that all the effort was worthwhile.

INTENDED FOR PLEASURE

Marriage should be a pleasurable experience. God placed within man and woman a desire for the opposite sex. The physical desire for sex is good and it is God given. God intended men and women to enjoy this wonderful experience; however God has outlined certain guidelines to be followed. Adultery and fornication are prohibited and damaging to a marriage. The intimate relationship of a couple is so strong that it must be guarded and nurtured. Sex is the ultimate expression of love that two people share in the most intimate relationship by becoming one, physically and emotionally. Without love sex becomes selfish and results in guilt and shame. When sex is the result of sacrificial love, it is a holy experience.

The animal world has sex merely for procreation. Humans are unique in that sex is for personal enjoyment and emotional development, as well as for procreation. A healthy physical relationship will draw a couple closer together. Without the proper relationship it becomes merely a means to personal satisfaction. Your marriage union should be the greatest expression of love as you give yourself to your spouse unreservedly.

The enjoyment of sin for a season is nothing more than hedonism. God desires for us to be happy and healthy, but we must learn happiness is a result of living within the bounds God has set. He doesn't want people to be unhappy and drudge through life with a martyr complex. Laughter, joy, and happiness are all emotions God intends for marriage. Ask yourself, "When was the last time I enjoyed laughter in my home?" When was the last time you eagerly anticipated arriving home after a hard day of work? If not recently, I hope it will happen today.

STAYING IN LOVE

Every new marriage begins without experience. How can a couple expect to have a happy home when they don't know what to do? There isn't even a marriage manual to solve daily problems. An interesting paradox concerning marriage is that the very thing that destroys one home seems to strengthen another. An illness or a lost job is a common occurrence that can cause strain on a home. One couple allows the problem to separate them, while another couple uses the struggle to draw them closer together. There must be the right mindset when facing trials. A trial can draw a couple closer together or it can separate them—it all depends on their attitude.

When a home is established on commitment, there is always the attitude that we will do whatever is required to solve our problems.

I am thankful for a committed wife. My wife, Janet, could never have comprehended what was in store by marrying me. On our first anniversary we went on a survey trip to the Northeast to find a location to start a church. Not what one would consider a second honeymoon. On our anniversary we stayed overnight in the home of the parents of a college friend. However, in spite of some sacrifices there have been many special blessings and rewards. Just four days after our first anniversary, on a snowy Christmas Eve, we needed to stop for the night. I realized we were near Niagara Falls so we drove to the falls where we found only one other couple was registered in the entire motel. The next morning we visited a spectacular scene of fresh snow covering the falls and the surrounding area.

When a home is established on commitment, there is always the attitude that we will do whatever is required to solve our problems. When a marriage is built on emotion and selfishness, facing problems can very difficult. Anyone can become infatuated with a person; however infatuation is not enough to keep husbands and wives content through difficult times. The foundation of the home and the mindset at the time of matrimony are essential to the future happiness of a home.

Every young couple I have counseled for marriage has anticipated a happy and fulfilling future. Some come into my office walking on top of the clouds, while they are in a fog of infatuation. Often the wedding rehearsal requires perseverance to get their attention long enough to practice the ceremony. It is impossible for them to believe their marriage could ever be eroded by life's daily challenges. Yet, the pressures of life, the mundane routines, and family pressures can dampen the spark so that the flame dims and they return to my office seeking counsel they never expected to need. Marriage requires more work than most couples anticipate.

So what will keep the honey in the honeymoon? The obvious answer is a commitment to keep the marriage strong. Just how that is accomplished has many answers and they all require time and commitment. Time must be set aside for dating. I am not a big fan of teenage dating; however I am a very big fan of married couples' dating. The responsibility of marriage requires each person to fulfill the role God has given them, and to do so fervently. Many suggestions can be offered of special things to do and a few are suggested in Appendix #3.

LITTLE THINGS

Marital strife usually comes from a series of little things. Not placing clothes in the hamper, tracking dirt into a clean house, or failure to repair a leaky faucet can perturb any wife. Unprepared meals, failure to dress attractively, complaining, and a lack of encouragement can discourage any husband. Divorce often occurs as a result of several little things that were neglected over a long period of time. I realize there can be other, more relevant issues that bring great heartache, but

Consider your relationship over the past year and honestly ask yourself, what have I done to enhance my relationship with my spouse?

often separation and divorce occur from a lack of attention to little things. Life is made up of little things. Notes, flowers, and cards can create an amazing change in a marriage. A special meal or pampering can bring great delight to an unsuspecting spouse. Consider your relationship over the past year and honestly ask yourself, what have I done to enhance my relationship with my spouse? If you have done very little then it is no wonder the marriage has lost its excitement.

Wrong authority and structure will always hinder the home from becoming God's best, but little things will gradually have the same effect if left unattended. All the things a young couple would do while dating should really be seen as relevant to marriage. Kind words, a show of affection, kind deeds, encouraging words, and frequent surprises all will enhance a marriage. Speaking unkind words, arguing, and proving you are right never helps a relationship. Forgiveness, understanding, compassion, and encouragement make more sense if you want to build your marriage.

Marriage can be hell on earth or heaven on earth. The kind of home you have is determined by what you do to build it. The dividends of following the Bible are priceless, and all of these blessings are available to every couple. The choice is yours; why not decide to make your home the greatest thing in the world?

My Hope Chest Is Full

CHAPTER FOUR

Precious Memories

The days of our engagement were wonderful times. I had proposed to my bride-to-be, she said yes, and the dreams and hopes of our own home were soon to be realized. We were Bible College students, preparing for the ministry and we had only a two-week window between semesters to be married and enjoy a brief honeymoon before returning to school to finish our final exams. Those six months prior to our wedding were filled with endless talk concerning our dreams and future plans. Our earnest desire was to please the Lord and our plans were guided by His will.

The night before our wedding an unusually powerful December snow storm dropped seventeen inches of snow. Our rehearsal was cancelled and held the same day as the wedding. Guests had difficulty arriving and some never dared to try. The ceremony was held as scheduled and our lives began a unique journey. We had secured the use of a house trailer on a small lake near our home, but upon arrival I found the entrance completely covered and impassable. I asked my wife to hold on as I drove the car into the snow bank where it stayed for a few days. I then carried my new bride up the drive through the snow to our retreat.

Our future offered hope that was untested, but very real. While knowing there would be difficult times, we anticipated a bright and wonderful future, because our faith was in God. Through faith we trusted in the God of the universe to lead us on a plain path. We understood marriage is a serious commitment, and we recognized our need of divine intervention. Many positive influences providentially enabled us to establish a truly Christian home. Our parents, our Bible College, teachers, our church, and our friends all contributed to the early stages of our marriage.

Marriage is difficult under the best of circumstances. I can't imagine starting a home without God's divine guidance. The following years have brought trials and testing along with joys and blessings. Our faith that God's way is best has not changed. Often people will comment, "You have such a wonderful family." No greater compliment could be given as those dreams and hopes of the future have been realized. All the honor must go to our Savior, who has led us through these years.

Is Your Hope Chest Full?

A hope chest is a wonderful gift parents can give to a newly engaged daughter. Often the hope chest is cedar, and it's typically a large, wooden box built specifically to contain special items ideally suited for one soon to be married. Parents can use this chest to store dishes and linens, and to pass on heirlooms of sentimental importance. The tradition provides a means whereby a young girl can dream of her future. With every towel comes the dream that soon she will be able to dry the dishes and clean the counters of her own home. The heirloom dishes will provide many future memories of entertaining and perhaps special nights of dining alone with her husband. The process of planning and dreaming of a new home soon becomes her primary purpose and focus for the coming months. The hopes and dreams of a loving marriage and children conceived from their love all provide promise and hope for the future.

Not every new bride has a literal hope chest. However, the hopes and dreams of a happy home are still the hopes of every new bride-to-be. As a hope chest provides necessary utensils and articles to operate a home, so the necessary ingredients for emotional and spiritual success are equally important. Beginning with childhood and until the time of marriage, life is much like a hope chest. The ingredients must be put in to insure that the young bride will bring the necessary things to the new home. Every day in the life of a child is a time of preparation for that day. Wise parents will teach their children to prepare for that day. The development of character is an essential item that must not be excluded. The years of spiritual, emotional, and physical development are crucial to the future blessedness of the soon-to-be home. Don't delay putting the right things into your life to prepare you for the special times that lie ahead. Hopefully, your hope chest will be full when the time comes for your marriage. May your hope chest fill you with joy and hope, regardless of its actual appearance. May it fill you with hope for the future, as you keep your eyes on Jesus while He seeks out your future husband. Let this be a time of joyful preparation for your high calling as a future wife and mother.

THE RIGHT WAY IN MARRIAGE

In Mark 10:7-9, Jesus teaches that a man is to leave his father and mother in order to establish his own home. "For this cause shall a man leave his father and mother, and cleave to his wife; and they twain shall be one flesh: so then they are no more twain, but one flesh. What therefore God hath joined together, let not man put asunder." Every new home has the opportunity to be built on God's Word. Even if parents failed to have a happy home, a newly married couple can break the bonds of the past if they will follow biblical teaching. A marriage will not take care of itself: A couple must make a conscious choice to build a home on God's Word.

Building a God-honoring home begins with the choice of a spouse. Finding the right mate is an ominous task that should not be taken lightly. The typical young adult today has little knowledge of the Biblical perspective in finding their life partner. Today's American custom of dating is full of many dangerous pitfalls. Following the typical worldly system is a dangerous decision that can lead to certain heartache. Consider how Isaac and Rebecca grieved over their son Esau's relationship with the daughters of Heth. And Esau was forty years old when he took to wife Judith, the daughter of Beeri the Hittite, and Bashemath the daughter of Elon the Hittite, choices that brought grief to Isaac and Rebekah (see Genesis 26:34-35). "And Rebekah said to Isaac, I am weary of my life because of the daughters of Heth: if Jacob take a wife of the daughters of Heth, such as these which are of the daughters of the land, what good shall my life do me?" (Genesis 27:46).

Refusing the counsel of parents is dangerous and usually results in disaster.

Samson is another example of opposing parental guidance. God used his improper relationship for good, but it could not be considered a wise decision:

> "Then his father and his mother said unto him, Is there never a woman among the daughters of thy brethren, or among all my people, that thou goest to take a wife of the uncircumcised Philistines? And Samson said unto his father, Get her for me; for she pleaseth me well" (Judges 14:3).

Refusing the counsel of parents is dangerous and usually results in disaster. Seeking godly counsel is the wisest thing a prospective couple can do. During the teen and early adult years sexual interest is extremely high and young people need to be informed and prepared for this emotional change in their life. Pushing a child to mature prematurely can be emotionally disastrous. Little girls need to be allowed to be little girls and boys need to be allowed to be boys. Sexual experimentation does not help prepare anyone for marriage; rather it creates emotional scars that can last a lifetime. Parents can establish a wall of protection around their children. Wise rules should be established and taught to children early in their lives (Appendix #1). "But fornication, and all uncleanness, or covetousness, let it not be once named among you, as becometh saints" (Ephesians 5:3).

Other than the decision to receive Christ as your Savior, your decision of who you will marry is the greatest decision you will make.

Parents have a great responsibility to protect and prepare their children to stand on their own. Permitting a young couple to be alone at home or in a car unattended spells danger. It is not only dangerous, it is also cruel. Teens or young adults who think they know how to handle their emotions are deceiving themselves. Anyone considering marriage should welcome godly advice with open arms.

Marriage Is a Big Decision

Other than the decision to receive Christ as your Savior, your decision of who you will marry is the greatest decision you will make. You must recognize that God has a perfect plan for your life right now, and as you daily follow His plan He will lead you to the right way in marriage. Your circumstances and relationships are all orchestrated by God's hand.

An important criterion for finding the right spouse is to be dedicated to God's will. Living in His will enhances your opportunity to find the right person to marry, and it will cause you to wait upon the Lord by allowing Him to provide you with His best. Remember, God's best is always your best. Our great God desires the best for your life, and you should never settle for anything less.

My oldest daughter, Elizabeth graduated from college and returned home to teach in our Christian school. Although many fine young men attended her college she complained there just wasn't anyone there she would ever consider for marriage. Her future husband Barnabas had recently graduated from an even larger Bible College and complained to his parents, there just wasn't anyone at school he would ever consider for marriage. One day Barney delivered some stone to our dormitory construction site and from the moment I met him I felt he was the one for my daughter, though I never mentioned it to anyone. A few months later on a mission trip they surprisingly were seated on the same flight where they became acquainted. From that trip a relationship developed that explained why there was no one they would marry while in college, their future mate was not in their college. They both still are curious how they ended up being seated together on that flight. Today they are happily serving the Lord in full time ministry. Consider that most of your years on this earth will probably be spent married to your life partner. Your entire future will be influenced by whom you marry. Your children, in-laws, and relatives all will be determined by your marriage choice. It's no exaggeration to say that your future happiness will be determined by this great decision of marriage. No one should enter into holy matrimony without recognizing the importance of this decision.

When Should You Get Married?

During the middle of the twentieth century it was not unusual for a teen girl to leave high school and be married. In many cases these girls did so with their parents' approval. That was then and this is now! Sixty years ago young girls knew how to run a home and had the character to do it. Today a seventeen-year-old girl will not be prepared for the responsibility of marriage. Some young girls think that if they have graduated from high school and have no prospects of marriage they are an old maid. Eighteen, twenty-one, thirty, or fifty-five are arbitrary ages. Although most people marry in their twenties, many are now postponing marriage until later in life. Age is not the only factor to consider in marriage. Although marriage is for unbelievers as well as believers, Christians should only seek marriage when they have been prepared by their family to follow the way of the Lord.

The most important factor for a Christian is to marry a fellow believer. Don't be unequally yoked (2 Corinthians 6:14). It isn't unusual for a young man who becomes emotionally involved with a Christian girl to agree to attend church and claim he believes in God. However, the basis of any union should be to marry only a dedicated Christian. Even when a person is dedicated there are many factors that should be considered. Are they seeking the same calling as you? Do they have a similar background and culture? God will bless a couple when they have the right motives and goals.

- "Meats for the belly, and the belly for meats: but God shall destroy both it and them. Now the body is not for fornication, but for the Lord; and the Lord for the body" (1 Corinthians 6:13).
- "The wife is bound by the law as long as her husband liveth; but if her husband be dead, she is at liberty to be married to whom she will; only in the Lord" (1 Corinthians 7:39).

Certain things are necessary to properly enter into marriage:

1. Finding the right person.
2. The maturity to respect and heed the advice of your parents.
3. The financial ability to live independently from your parents.
4. The ability to commit sufficient time to the marriage
5. Basic skills to function in society.

Behold, the Camels are Coming

"And Isaac went out to meditate in the field at the eventide: and he lifted up his eyes, and saw, and, behold, the camels were coming" (Genesis 24:63). Isaac had anticipated this moment for quite some time, and what an exciting event it must have been. The first meeting of Rebekah and Isaac had to be a spectacle to behold. Isaac had gone out into the field to meditate, and he looked up and saw the camels were coming. Rebekah had been riding a camel for several days and must have known she was drawing close when suddenly she looked up and saw Isaac. Then she jumped off her camel to meet him. God brought together two young lives, and through their union all the world would be blessed.

God has a plan concerning marriage for every young person and waiting for His plan is a wise decision.

God has a plan concerning marriage for every young person and waiting for His plan is a wise decision. Waiting on God for marriage requires faith, just like any other aspect of the Christian life. Begin by surrendering your life to His will. The most important people who can help you make the right decision are God, your parents, and your pastor. Never fear godly counsel, because it is your best friend.

The principles of finding the right partner are countless; however a few are very definable and precise:

1. *Marry only in the Lord*
   a. Only a Christian
   b. Only a dedicated Christian
   c. Only a dedicated Christian with the same goals in life
2. *Seek godly counsel*
   a. Parents are the greatest resource
   b. Pastoral guidance is important
   c. Godly family or friends can provide good advice

3. *Pray*
    a. Pray daily for God's leading
    b. Pray for God to prepare you
    c. Pray for assurance and peace
4. *Get your confidence from the Holy Spirit*
    a. The relationship makes you stronger spiritually
    b. Peace and confidence reins in your heart
    c. Godly influences confirm decisions
5. *Have similar desires and plans*
    a. Your calling
    b. Your lifestyle
    c. Your culture
6. *Have the same convictions*
    a. Biblical standards
        1. Music
        2. Dress
        3. Associations
    b. Rearing children
    c. Church
7. *Be transparent*
    a. Honesty
    b. Intimacy
    c. Encouragement

Unequally Yoked

"Be ye not unequally yoked together with unbelievers: for what fellowship hath righteousness with unrighteousness? and what communion hath light with darkness?" (2 Corinthians 6:14). Paul's message to the Corinthians pertained to every aspect of life in which an alliance with unbelievers would compromise their personal faith in Christ. Although the text refers to many aspects of daily life, it especially refers to marriage. Throughout Bible times God required His people to refrain from intermarriage with unbelievers, and that has not changed, even now in our modern times. Many a young bride has compromised this truth only to pay a great price later for her disobedience. Countless ladies and men have explained to me their remorse for marrying a nonbeliever. The organist at my wedding explained to my wife how happy she was to play for our wedding, because she had hoped one day to be a missionary, but made the mistake of marrying a man who never attended church with her, thus dashing any hope of fulfilling her God given desire of becoming a missionary. She found solace in helping us to follow the Lord. Another sad situation involved a pastor who recently started a church and became a great support and blessing to our ministry. I was saddened to learn his wife called him from the airport and demanded he come with her immediately or she would leave him and never return. That good man of God had to resign his church and leave the ministry. I could fill a few books with the tragic stories of marriages united without a common bond.

The expectation of every Christian man and woman should be to marry only someone who is saved and living a consistent Christian life. Every Christian must hold to their convictions and marry only someone with the same beliefs and convictions. Don't be blinded by infatuation. No one should compromise by finding a spouse who is not consistently living for the Lord and actively serving in a Bible-believing church.

Paul specifically had the following things in mind when he wrote the church at Corinth to warn them of being unequally yoked.

- *Idolatry:* This was plain; Christians were not to entangle themselves with idolatry. The early disciples refused to cast incense on the altar of a pagan god, and because they refused many perished as martyrs.

- *Sin:* Christians are in no way to participate in the sins common to man, but to be separate from the world.

- *Acts of dishonesty and deception:* No believer should involve himself with the dishonest deeds of another; even if it is your employer. Any business partner or employer that requires a Christian to sin is requiring an unholy alliance.

- *Marriage:* The marriage of a Christian to an unbeliever is strictly forbidden, and for good reason. How can the two cooperate in the rearing of children, the attendance and support of the church, and the basic aspects of daily life? In situations where salvation occurs after marriage, remaining with an unbelieving spouse is encouraged by scripture. And the woman which hath an husband that believeth not, and if he be pleased to dwell with her, let her not leave him. (1 Corinthians 7:13) A believing spouse has a special opportunity to reach their partner by personal testimony and living in a godly manner.

There are Biblical ways in which Christians may interact with unbelievers that do not compromise beliefs and convictions.

- *Business transactions* and employment that are conducted in an honest fashion.
- *Public pursuits* that do not interfere with biblical principles. Medical and humanitarian deeds for the benefit of society are fully understandable and commendable, provided they do not compromise the Word of God.
- *Family and relatives.* An adult is always obligated to honor his parents, because of their position. Respect should be passed on to children so as to train them to honor their parents.
- *Our government.* A Christian is obligated to certain duties of paying taxes, voting, serving or supporting our military, and many other civic duties that do not violate Scripture.
- *Witnessing to the lost.* Making friends for the sake of the gospel is quite different from making friends with the world to enjoy their amusements. We are commanded to go into the world and preach the gospel. "And of some have compassion, making a difference" (Jude 1:22).

Every young person dreams of their future home. They visualize a nice suburban home, a wonderful husband, and happy healthy children. No one intends to be divorced or for their children to become drug addicts or criminals. The hopes and dreams can be realized with the proper actions. My pastor and his wife greatly enhanced our home by their counsel. Listening to our parents and reading books on marriage enhanced our ability to fulfill our dreams. A hope chest can become more than hope; it can become a reality to be passed on to the next generation.

Is your hope chest full?

"Wisdom has built her house: she has hewn out her seven pillars" (Proverbs 9:1).

Money Is Not Your Problem

CHAPTER FIVE

Precious Memories

Setting up a budget soon after marriage was not a project my new bride was eager to tackle. She was not accustomed to living on such a low income. I recall detailing how every penny would be allocated. We literally couldn't buy a piece of chewing gum unless it was allocated in our budget. Our simple system required strict restraint. My wife was cooperative, but not enthusiastic about our seemingly monastic lifestyle.

After a few months had passed I mentioned to Janet that enough money was in our clothing fund to purchase her a new dress. Her response was that we couldn't afford it. I assured her the money was in fact in the fund and had no other purpose but to purchase clothing. Reluctantly, she allowed me to drive her to the mall and we looked at a few dresses until she found one to her liking. We bought the dress and she was elated about it. Soon we made other purchases in the same fashion, all to her liking. In fact she became very persistent about strictly following our budget. Our meager income did not become a hindrance to our happiness. We both look back at those times with great appreciation.

MONEY PROBLEMS

The title of this chapter may sound strange, but the truth is, money problems are really behavior problems. Money may receive the blame, but the problem is in the decisions we make about our possessions. People often mistakenly believe if they had more income their financial issues would disappear. If they could just win the lottery they would be on easy street.

People often mistakenly believe if they had more income their financial issues would disappear.

Unfortunately, this is not the case. In fact, studies have shown just the opposite. Lottery winners' newly acquired fortune soon turned to misery, resulting in divorce, bankruptcy and, sadly, sometimes ending in suicide.

Money is necessary in this world. Money is not evil, nor is it a god; it is simply a tool. Rightly understanding it and respecting Biblical principles concerning its use is the emphasis of this chapter. Learning to be content with the blessings God gives you is the key. The Biblical principles necessary are: (1) Learning to live within your means (2) Not becoming entangled with the world and (3) Learning to make money your servant not your master. "Not that I speak in respect of want: for I have learned, in whatsoever state I am, therewith to be content" (Philippians 4:11).

YOUR MINDSET

I remember a preacher once said, "Giving is not a matter of can or can't, it is a matter of will or won't." Stewardship of our possessions is a personal decision; a matter of the will. As Christians we must realize we are stewards of 100 percent of our money, not merely 10 percent. All our possessions are really God's, and we are stewards of them. Our mindset determines our response to the great responsibility of caring for all the things over which God has made us caretakers.

Several years ago I knew a dear, elderly Polish lady who lived in an old house on the corner of a piece of prime real estate. Her clothes were fifty years old and she had no modern conveniences in her home. She lived as a pauper. Eventually her property was sold for a large sum of money and she moved to a rental apartment. Some time later, several ladies were helping her move out of the rental apartment because the landlord has just raised the rent by a meager amount. I felt the rent hike was reasonable, but this lady was determined she would not spend the extra money.

Resigned that her decision was firm, I asked some ladies to help her pack and we would move her to her new location. The few things she owned were old and most were really not worth keeping, but we tried to honor her wishes and pack whatever she asked us to move. In the afternoon the ladies called and asked me to hurry over. Upon arrival I was presented with two shoeboxes of money. The ladies were shaking for fear of being accused of taking the money. I quickly calculated that the boxes contained more than $100,000.

This lady refused to spend money. She had hundreds of thousands of dollars in the bank and thousands in cash in her closet. Why would she not spend the money or buy some new clothes? I am convinced she would not spend the money because she grew up in poverty and always had to be careful about her use of money. She was never able to change her behavior, even when she could have improved her lifestyle.

I recall another example that was exactly the opposite. This young couple was struggling financially, even though he had a good job and an excellent income. They came to me seeking counsel concerning their financial troubles. After asking a few questions I saw a pattern developing. They spent money like water. It was as though they opened their van window and threw money out of it.

This family had several thousands of dollars of debt and almost no assets. They rented an apartment, made payments on a van, and they were finding it hard to put food on the table. They had no savings or investments; only debt and credit cards. How did they get into such a mess? They gave me a long and detailed explanation, but it could be summarized by saying they had no restraint. They went from one thing to another buying whatever they thought they needed.

I tried to help them with a budget, but I remember they were not really interested in living the way their budget would require them to live. Later I told the husband I knew the answer to his problem. To his horror I stated, "I think you have too much money." Your problem is you need smaller numbers to work with so that you can learn to handle your money. Amazingly he did experience a severe cut in his income and he did respond better because of it. But it is extremely difficult to change poor money management styles.

CHANGE IS DIFFICULT

Changing your attitude toward money is not easy, especially when the situation requires restraint. Some people just can't seem to do it. They always justify their purchases and expenditures as necessary. The depth of one's commitment determines his ability to cut his budget and get out of debt. If a poor steward received a large sum of money I am convinced in a short time he would somehow find a way to spend it all,

The depth of one's commitment determines his ability to cut his budget and get out of debt.

resulting in a pile of new debt. A good steward could accept the debt of another and he would find a way to clear it up. The difference between the two is their mindset. A couple that is committed will say, "We can't afford bedroom furniture; we'll use donated furniture or we'll sleep on the floor." If their washer is broken and they can't afford the repair or can't afford to purchase a new one, they'll go to a Laundromat or wash their clothes in the bathtub. If their car breaks down they'll borrow a ride, walk, or ride a bike. If they can't pay their bills they'll work a second job. If that isn't enough, they'll work a third job or more if necessary. Those who have a proper mindset will make all adjustments necessary to fix the problem. There is no sacrifice too great to have a good testimony.

MONEY WORKS EXPONENTIALLY

The word exponential is an important word to understand. Exponentiation is a mathematical operation involving two numbers, the base a and the exponent n. When n is a whole number, exponentiation is repeated multiplication. Multiplication is repeated addition; exponential growth is far greater than multiplication. Wealth can grow exponentially, and debt also can grow exponentially. The most important element in financial growth and debt is time. I try to impress upon every young couple I counsel how simple it is to acquire an enormous retirement if they start immediately and continue for a long time. The longer people wait to begin saving, the harder it is to build sufficient savings. If you can't pay one month's rent for now, how will you pay two months rent next month? Debt can be extremely difficult to remove, and the longer it remains the more it enslaves you.

Today's greatest financial tragedy is the use of credit cards. At the moment you assume you can make the payments, so you purchase something that may not be necessary. When you reach a point that you can't make your payments it can quickly spiral downward. A simple rule should be to never purchase anything with a credit card unless you already have the money in the bank to pay the bill when it arrives. I know for some the wheels are turning and you have several reasons why this cannot be true. But there can be no exceptions. If you don't have the money to pay for it then you must not purchase it.

BUDGET IS NOT A BAD WORD

The mere mention of the word budget causes paralysis in the minds of some people. I have heard some strange comments about budgets. I have been told, "I can't afford to set up a budget." Others have said, "I don't have enough money to set up a budget." No doubt many have felt a budget will not help them. However, anyone in debt or living on a small income must, must, must have a budget.

There are many types of budgets, but a budget must involve restraint, and it must be followed to achieve success. Computers provide the ability to track finances in great detail and with relative ease. But that does not mean anyone in debt should immediately run to the store to buy a computer, thinking it has the answer to their financial woes. All you may find is more debt from your purchase. A budget is of no value unless it is followed.

The proper use of a budget can be illustrated by a shoebox. Assemble several shoeboxes and label them by categories of expenses. Utilities, rent, groceries, giving, clothing, auto expenses, insurance, medical, repair, and recreation are all examples of typical categories of expense. When a paycheck is received a predetermined budget amount is assigned to each box. The entire paycheck should be cashed and the cash placed in the appropriate box. Every bill must be paid entirely from the assigned box for that particular category. If money is not present in a particular box then an item must not be purchased and money must not be borrowed from another box.

The reason many people continue in debt is because they continually borrow from one shoebox to pay for the expense of another shoebox that doesn't have the necessary funds to make the purchase. By their lack of discipline they are continually behind in paying their bills. If money is not available for a certain category, then purchasing the item must be put off until the money is available. Your tithe, food and other categories may remain at zero at the end of each week. However other categories will begin to build a balance. It is difficult to start, but it can be done, even with no cash reserves; just start with the first paycheck. Learning to live by this restraint will encourage you to find another means of solving your financial problems. Refusal to do so will result in financial ruin.

In the process of developing this new budget you may initially experience a time of discouragement. You will probably even have a pity party and be tempted to quit. You are experiencing withdrawal, just like a drug addict or alcoholic. You must resist the urge to quit, and determine to stay with your plan, regardless of the sacrifice required. You will soon begin to realize the terrible effect these past tendencies have had on your life. If you remain faithful you will soon be rewarded for your effort. If this doesn't work, you may have to resort to seeking the help of a trusted friend or adviser until you resolve your problems.

The proper understanding of the use of money is the responsibility of every Christian.

Of course, the same type of budget can be implemented by using a computer as a budget book. However, I must again remind you the budget itself will do nothing for you, unless you determine to follow this simple program. Getting out of debt and paying your bills is something to which every Christian must aspire. However, there is much more to stewardship that learning to pay your bills in a timely fashion. Planning for the future is also an important aspect of money management for every believer. Savings should be allotted for major purchases such as a home, college for your children, a car, or retirement. The proper understanding of the use of money is the responsibility of every Christian.

Making a Million

I insist on four counseling meetings with every couple seeking marriage. One of the sessions involves finances. Although making a million dollars should not be the goal of a Christian, being a good steward should. Three real-life examples illustrate the significance of good stewardship.

Couple number 1

Married at age twenty-four, they spend all their wedding money on the wedding and honeymoon. They use credit cards to purchase furniture and clothing. They finance both their cars for four years. They continue to spend more than they make, but their two incomes allow them to make the payments on their bills but only for a time. Soon they fail to make their payments while discovering she is expecting. They now have $20,000 of debt at 18 percent interest. The monthly payment is $300, and that's not even paying a penny on principle. They lose her income. They now begin to sacrifice and only find more bills coming and the costs becoming greater. They can't tithe, and they can't save. Perhaps, over several years they'll learn their lesson and get out of debt, or perhaps they'll never fully recover. At age sixty-five they have a car payment, own no home, have no investments, and are dependent on social security, on others, or on a small pension. Their total savings is a few dollars in their checking account.

Couple number 2

Also married at age twenty-four, they save half of their wedding money, and she works while they live on his salary for one year. At the end of one year they have $20,000. At age twenty-five they invest the $20,000 at the rate of 10 percent. Each year they invest another $500. At age sixty-five (forty years later) their nest egg will have grown to one million dollars. If they could invest this money with a return of 10 percent, their yearly income from this alone would be $100,000.

Couple number 3

A retired pastor, now eighty years old, has a wife in a nursing home. The pastor never made more than $8,000.00 per year. The man's wife had saved $250,000, which she invested in an interest-bearing certificate of deposit. In addition, the pastor saved $350,000, which he placed in a savings account. The preacher also had stock worth over one million dollars. Their net cash value was $1,663,000. The man had no debt, because he never felt they could afford it.

Understanding the "Rule of 72" can be eye opening. Money invested at a certain interest rate divided into 72 will give you the number of years it takes to double. Example:

72 divided by 12 percent equals six years to double in value. Through this simple technique you can easily see how your money will work for you if you are wise.

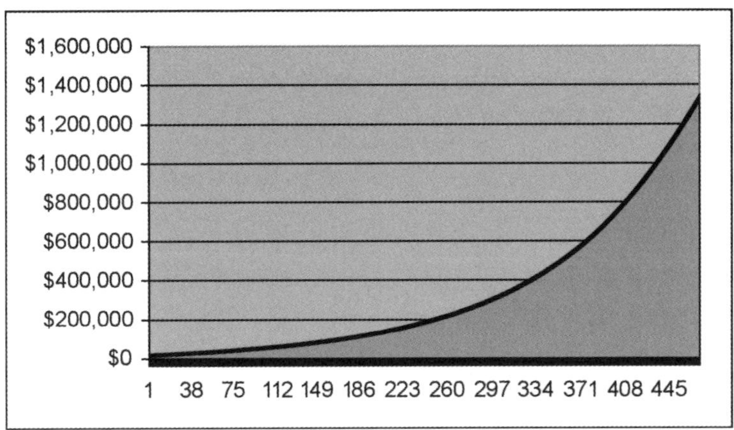

What kind of financial goals do you have? Are you concerned about your children's education? The only help I gave my children in college is the guidance they received while they were growing with us. Each child was required to save half of their Christmas money, birthday money, or earned money. I helped them to invest their money, and by the time they went to college they had enough money to pay for a good portion of their school bill. When they were old enough to get a job, we encouraged them to begin working and saving. I never gave my children a penny for college, yet each one graduated with no debt. In fact they all had acquired quite a surplus by the time they graduated.

If a child had no financial assistance and worked during the summer before attending college and saved his money he would only be required to work 25 hours a week in order to stay current with his school bill. It can be done if the proper principles are applied.

- The Christian's goal should not be prosperity, but to please God (see Matthew 6:33).
- The problem is that people want more than they need (covetousness).
- Some people feel they deserve more than they have (lack of gratitude).
- The result can be putting self before God (selfishness).

BENEVOLENCE

- "I have shewed you all things, how that so labouring ye ought to support the weak, and to remember the words of the Lord Jesus, how he said, It is more blessed to give than to receive" (Acts 20:35).
- "Give, and it shall be given unto you; good measure, pressed down, and shaken together, and running over, shall men give into your bosom. For with the same measure that ye mete withal it shall be measured to you again" (Luke 6:38).

Every believer should have a giving attitude. Husbands and wives should give to each other, and parents should learn to give to their children. Neighbors should know how to give to each other, and giving our best to the Lord brings our highest satisfaction. Our giving should not be motivated by expectations of financial remuneration. We should be willing to give, even if we receive nothing in return. A great by-product of giving is that many times God blesses us with unexpected benefits, but even without receiving these benefits we should be willing to give, simply to honor the Lord.

The Bible teaches us that it is more blessed to give than to receive.

The Bible teaches us that it is more blessed to give than to receive. This wonderful truth has been illustrated over and over again. What a joy to help someone in need. Our celebration of Christmas is a celebration of giving. One of the sad realities of poor stewardship is that it limits one's ability to give. I remember a man saying to me, "I wish I had a million dollars; I would give to the Lord's work." The man was disappointed he couldn't give to a needy cause and the reason was he had been a poor steward. God graciously gives to us so that we can give to others. God gave the ultimate gift of His Son so that we might have life. We would be poor Christians if we didn't endeavor to share that gift with others. "What shall we then say to these things? If God be for us, who can be against us? He that spared not his own Son, but delivered him up for us all, how shall he not with him also freely give us all things?" (Romans 8:31-32).

- *We should give cheerfully and willingly.* "Every man according as he purposeth in his heart, so let him give; not grudgingly, or of necessity: for God loveth a cheerful giver" (2 Corinthians 9:7).

- *We should give sacrificially, even in trial and poverty.* "How that in a great trial of affliction the abundance of their joy and their deep poverty abounded unto the riches of their liberality. For to their power, I bear record, yea, and beyond their power they were willing of themselves" (2 Corinthians 8:2-3).

MONEY IS A TOOL

Contentment with Godliness should be the goal of every home. There is nothing wrong with having money; it's a necessity in our society. Money is a tool God has given us to honor Him as we follow Biblical principles. But money also can be dangerous if we fail to understand its purpose. The amount of income is not the secret to happiness; rather it is one's attitude toward money and how it is handled that matters the most. I have observed families with limited incomes who contentedly meet all their basic needs. They are faithful to tithe, and never seem to struggle with finances. On the other hand, I have seen families with much greater incomes that are always in debt, struggling to pay their bills, unfaithful in giving to the Lord's work, and fighting over their finances. What is the difference? One family recognizes that money is merely a tool, while the other family believes it to be an end in itself.

Three basic financial principles must be understood to find success.

The first Biblical principle a new Christian must learn is contentment. We must learn to be content with the things we have. We live in a society that is always lusting after more and more possessions. Advertisers play on these feelings and appeal to the greed and envy of our old nature. We see something and we want it. I believe God wants to supply our needs and even our desires, but we must learn to be content and to be thankful for God's supply. Then we must be patient when we want something. Selfish desires will lead us down a path of entanglement that is filled with sorrow. Through the power of the Holy Spirit we can be content. Learn to recognize the things in life that really matter, such as your family, good health, and a good reputation.

> "But godliness with contentment is great gain. For we brought nothing into this world, and it is certain we can carry nothing out. And having food and raiment let us be therewith content. But they that will be rich fall into temptation and a snare, and into many foolish and hurtful lusts, which drown men in destruction and perdition. For the love of money is the root of all evil: which while some coveted after, they have erred from the faith, and pierced themselves through with many sorrows. But thou, O man of God, flee these things; and follow after righteousness, godliness, faith, love, patience, meekness" (1 Timothy 6:6-11).

The second important financial principle we must learn is restraint. This can be the most difficult lesson of all. We should never buy anything without having the funds to pay for it. Credit cards are a very convenient way to purchase things. However, if we don't have the money in a cash account to pay for something, we shouldn't buy it. A credit card with a high interest rate is a bad strategy and presumes upon the future.

That is how people get into trouble. A country saying expresses this truth well: "Once the horse is out of the barn it's hard to get him back in."

Many people think they are the exception. Perhaps there are a few exceptions, but over and over again I find people borrowing unnecessarily and rarely was it really an emergency with no alternative. What if your washer breaks down? Go to a Laundromat until you have the money to buy a new washing machine. What if your car breaks down? You can share a ride, ride the bus, or buy a cheaper car. But often people go for the sizzle. They buy the deal advertised on TV. No money down and a low monthly payment for six years. Then you find out the deal wasn't as good as it seemed. Later that dream becomes a burden because you are still making payments on a car that is worn out. Exercising restraint in the present pays great dividends in the future.

The third principle is investment. Investment is for those who are out of debt and paying their bills on time. Investing is a powerful tool. Remember that the goal should be contentment, not wealth. God can make us wealthy if He desires to do so, but our goal should be to properly handle the money God has given us. The most important element in investing is time. Proverbs 22:7 warns of a compulsive lifestyle: "The rich ruleth over the poor, and the borrower is servant to the lender."

Even the investment of our Christian service requires time. The longer the time of our investment the greater will be the return. This principle is a compelling argument to give our lives to serve the Lord while we are young. The same is true with money. The longer the investment is made, the greater the return will be. Many people are surprised with the amount of return when given enough time. If you have ever studied the yield curve on investments you will know that the last few years give the greatest amount of yield. This is called exponential growth. If every young person began saving and investing 5 percent of their yearly income they would be millionaires by age sixty-five. In fact, many would be multimillionaires. However, waiting until ten years prior to retirement yields a paltry retirement. Allowing only a few years for money to grow will result in disappointment.

One of the key elements in attaining financial freedom is learning to live by a budget.

Proper discipline regarding money is a key issue. A lack of training and discipline can result in financial ruin. One of the key elements in attaining financial freedom is learning to live by a budget. A budget can help provide restraint and planning. The purpose off a budget is not to bring discouragement, but success. If you want to learn how to invest you must first learn to use restraint.

I recall helping a young Christian family who was struggling with many personal problems. When I learned they were about to lose their home, I went to the bank and helped them develop a plan to save their home. As I reviewed their finances, it became clear they could set up a budget that would work for them, if they would follow through. When they saw they had enough money to pay their bills, I anticipated they would be excited to know they would be able to keep their home. I also expected to receive wonderful accolades for my financial counsel. I will never forget their response to my suggested plan. "You don't expect us to live like that, do you?" The problem was not that they lacked money; they lacked the desire to place restraint as a priority above their immediate wants. They owned horses, which were a great expense to house and feed. They refused to give up their horses, but they were willing to give up their home. If we develop such a strong desire for a godly home that our job, our hobbies and our personal satisfaction are secondary, we have taken another step toward achieving a happy home. Anyone who says, "You don't expect me live like that, do you," reveals to me their misplaced priorities.

THE GOSPEL OF PROSPERITY

God promised to make Abraham a great nation. The Patriarchs and other Old Testament believers were promised God's blessing, which often produced wealth as well as well-being. Should a good Christian expect wealth as a result of obedience to the Lord? Many televangelists give the impression Christians will become wealthy if they follow their agenda. Consider the faithful men and women who became first-century martyrs. Were they successful? While they are commended as great men and women of faith, they were never prosperous in the world's eyes. It would be presumptuous to assume we should become wealthy as a result of our faithfulness to God. Job said, "Naked came I out of my mother's womb, and naked shall I return thither: the LORD gave, and the LORD hath taken away; blessed be the name of the LORD" (Job 1:21).

Our goal should be to serve the Lord, whether by life or by death. We brought nothing into this world and we will take nothing with us when we die. Spiritual blessings are always superior to material ones, and one day we will receive our reward that will never fade or corrupt.

The idea of prosperity is always appealing to the flesh, but a man living in the Spirit will learn the importance of faithfulness, even in times of trial. Religious charlatans abound, seeking to deceive you into sending them your money with promises that you will become prosperous. The flesh delights in get-rich quick schemes, but God desires preeminence in our lives. Our purpose in life should never be determined by money, but by faith. The just shall live by faith. We are asked to live by faith, trusting our great God to supply every need.

- "But my God shall supply all your need according to his riches in glory by Christ Jesus" (Philippians 4:19).
- "But seek ye first the kingdom of God, and his righteousness; and all these things shall be added unto you. Take therefore no thought for the morrow: for the morrow shall take thought for the things of itself. Sufficient unto the day is the evil thereof" (Matthew 6:33-34).
- "No servant can serve two masters: for either he will hate the one, and love the other; or else he will hold to the one, and despise the other. Ye cannot serve God and mammon" (Luke 16:13).

Bible examples of financial failure:

- The rich man who hoarded his money (Luke 12:13-21).

- The prodigal son who wanted instant gratification (Luke 15:11).
- Achan, who took something God had cursed (Joshua 6:17-18).

"Go to now, ye that say, To day or to morrow we will go into such a city, and continue there a year, and buy and sell, and get gain: Whereas ye know not what shall be on the morrow. For what is your life? It is even a vapour, that appeareth for a little time, and then vanisheth away. For that ye ought to say, If the Lord will, we shall live, and do this, or that" (James 4:13-15).

Three principles we must learn concerning money

1. God owns it all.
2. Money is never an end in itself, but is merely a resource used to accomplish other goals and obligations.
3. Spend less than you earn, and do it for a long time.

Biblical Principles to Know and Understand

The most common money mistakes are a compulsive lifestyle and lack of a budget. We should study Bible principles in order to avoid these pitfalls. Take time to meditate upon these passages and allow them to penetrate your heart and mind.

- "A little that a righteous man hath is better than the riches of many wicked" (Psalm 37:16).

- "He that trusteth in his riches shall fall: but the righteous shall flourish as a branch" (Proverbs 11:28).
- "There is that maketh himself rich, yet hath nothing: there is that maketh himself poor, yet hath great riches" (Proverbs 13:7).
- "A good name is rather to be chosen than great riches, and loving favour rather than silver and gold" (Proverbs 22:1).

The most common money mistakes are a compulsive lifestyle and lack of a budget.

- "Labour not to be rich: cease from thine own wisdom" (Proverbs 23:4).
- "I returned, and saw under the sun, that the race is not to the swift, nor the battle to the strong, neither yet bread to the wise, nor yet riches to men of understanding, nor yet favour to men of skill; but time and chance happeneth to them all" (Ecclesiastes 9:11).
- "He also that received seed among the thorns is he that heareth the word; and the care of this world, and the deceitfulness of riches, choke the word, and he becometh unfruitful" (Matthew 13:22).
- "If therefore ye have not been faithful in the unrighteous mammon, who will commit to your trust the true riches?" (Luke 16:11).

- "Because thou sayest, I am rich, and increased with goods, and have need of nothing; and knowest not that thou art wretched, and miserable, and poor, and blind, and naked" (Revelation 3:17).

It has been reported that money is today's chief cause for divorce. I would like to challenge that statement by commenting it is the love and misuse of money and not money itself that brings turmoil to a home. True success is not measured by our wealth or power, but by the extent of God's control in our life. Whether wealthy or poor, it will matter not in eternity. "There is that maketh himself rich, yet hath nothing: there is that maketh himself poor, yet hath great riches" (Proverbs 13:7).

What riches cannot do...

"There are three things that earthly riches can never do — they can never satisfy divine justice, they can never pacify divine wrath, nor can they every quiet a guilty conscience. And until these things are done, man is undone."

THOMAS BROOKS

A House On The Sand

Chapter Six

Precious Memories

How well I remember the year of my fourth child's birth. Our growing church was in the midst of a building program, and I was not only the general contractor, but also I was doing much of the work. My pregnant wife was trying her best to be a good mother to our other three small children, while I was busy pastoring and building a new church building. Complications with the pregnancy caused my wife to be bedridden for the remainder of her term, which meant six months of bed rest. There was really no one to help us, so I prepared meals, cleaned the house, and dressed the children before I left my wife to deal as best she could with the melee soon to occur.

One day I returned home for lunch and found it impossible to enter our apartment. While my wife was napping our oldest son had found a box of yarn and made a spider's web that was suspended throughout the house. Every day was a unique adventure, and many times I was met with some new problem when I returned home. I took the children with me as often as possible and tried to help my wife and tend to the children, but this was a great strain upon our home, to say the least.

We both knew before our marriage there could be difficult experiences in the future, so before our wedding we decided to build our home on God's Word. Even though we knew trials would come, they still were difficult to face. Our trials could have caused some homes to be stressed to the point of collapse, but ours strengthened. Because we were building our home on the Lord, we found a solid rock in times of trouble. Everyone will face their own trials. But when the trials come it is important to be building your home on the rock.

YOU DON'T EXPECT ME TO STAY MARRIED TO HIM, DO YOU?

My wife listened intently as another woman described the awful plight of her friend, on the verge of divorce. A story soon developed, describing a man who was an awful husband, and if he was half as bad as he was being described, he belonged in prison. Upon completing the tirade of personal destruction the lady turned to my wife and asked, "You don't expect her to stay married to him do you?" My wife carefully questioned her informant, "She married him, didn't she?" If this man was as despicable as suggested, why did she enter into holy matrimony with such a vile person? If this wretch changed after their marriage why did she have so little influence to encourage him to be godly? It is easy to pass blame, but always difficult to admit.

At one time this couple stood at a marriage altar, pronounced their love for each other, and recited the words "till death do us part." No one forced or coerced them to get married; it was of their own volition. Somehow this marriage that once was filled with anticipation had deteriorated to the point of bitterness and anger. What did she see in him then? When two people fail to do their part in building a marriage the result is stress and unhappiness. What God had intended to be a heaven on earth has become a hell on earth, and now they are seeking excuses and someone to blame.

Every home that fails is an unhappy place. No one wants to live in a home filled with anger and strife; however the answer is to face the problems and correct them. Perhaps your home cannot be salvaged, but far too many have given up too soon without making the necessary effort to rebuild their relationship.

O, What a Tangled Web We Weave

Sir Walter Scott's poem, "O, what a tangled web we weave," could well apply to many homes today. Early in my ministry I learned a valuable lesson about how complicated families could become, and about the high price of disobedience. A young couple asked me to perform their marriage ceremony. I went to their home to counsel them and try to help them discover God's will in this possible union. I soon was given more information than I could decipher. It seems the woman had a child out of wedlock, after which she and this man had begun living together. Though not married, they had three children together, after which they separated and each married someone else. Later she became pregnant with yet another man's child, after which the couple moved back together. They recently had become Christians and now they felt they should be married and were seeking my help.

Their situation is one of those that fall under the category "What they never taught me in college." Honestly, I never received any advice in Bible College concerning a situation so complicated. I must say that I didn't have a clue of how to handle it, even though I knew God always has the answer. There is no situation so complicated that God does not have direction and hope, but I must warn you, the mistakes of the past cannot be erased, and sometimes the ramifications stay with you for a long time (Galatians 6:7). A dedicated Christian should seek to follow the Lord and not have to face such difficult situations.

God expects all people, Christian or not, to live by His laws, including marriage laws. Perhaps you were not saved at the time of your wedding. God still expected you to follow the biblical guidelines of marriage, and you will be held accountable to them. If you are legally married then the person you are married to is the right one for you! You should seek to please God in your home by living, to the best of your ability, the life God has given you. Marriage is a commitment of one man and one woman for life, and you are expected to obey God's Word and love your spouse. God can bless you in spite of your failures and in spite of your past mistakes. Romans 5:20 says, "Moreover the law entered, that the offence might abound. But where sin abounded, grace did much more abound." However, the next chapter of Romans states, "What shall we say then? Shall we continue in sin, that grace may abound? God forbid. How shall we, that are dead to sin, live any longer therein?" (Romans 6:1-2)

I Don't Love Him Anymore

The most common excuse I hear to justify divorce is, "The love is gone." We don't love each other anymore so we must do the right thing by divorcing rather than prolong an unhappy relationship. I have had Christians explain they know they should obey God and love their spouse, but their love would be fake and not spontaneous.

One of the most commonly misunderstood marital issues is that of emotional love. Why do emotional feelings exist during dating and then sometimes leave later in the marriage? The couple has confused emotional involvement with true love. How foolish to establish a home on something that can't possibly last. Obviously, the infatuation of a husband or wife will not continue forever. Building a relationship on infatuation is doomed to failure. Building a home on commitment, common goals, Biblical love, and trust will determine a couple's personal satisfaction and growth. Building a home on the proper virtues will result in happiness and contentment, while establishing a home on emotional feelings will eventually result in unhappiness and despair.

The Abhorrence of Immortality

"The beginning of the word of the LORD by Hosea. And the LORD said to Hosea, Go, take unto thee a wife of whoredoms and children of whoredoms: for the land hath committed great whoredom, departing from the LORD" (Hosea 1:2). The story of Hosea and his wife, Gomer, teach us of the beauty and grace of a godly home and the repulsiveness of an immoral one. God directed Hosea to marry Gomer, knowing she would play the harlot in Israel. Hosea must have suspected something was wrong from the very beginning. Attitudes such as Gomer's do not spring forth overnight. Every young man must learn to take heed if his prospective bride is overly concerned with her appearance, or if she is flirtatious. Gomer proved to be unfaithful soon after the marriage vows were repeated. She produced three children out of whoredom. The lesson from Hosea is one of love and grace, where great treachery and unfaithfulness existed. Adultery is vile, wicked, and ugly. God's grace can reach to lowest depths, but we must not forget results of immorality. God intends for His people to be pure and godly. The past can be forgiven, but we must turn from the old ways and seek to glorify God anew. Purity is vital to a happy and healthy home.

- "Ye adulterers and adulteresses know ye not that the friendship of the world is enmity with God? Whosoever therefore will be a friend of the world is the enemy of God" (James 4:4).
- "Marriage is honourable in all, and the bed undefiled: but whoremongers and adulterers God will judge" (Hebrews 13:4).

Consider the destructive nature of some of the evils of our day and how they can destroy something so wonderful as the home. Sin always destroys and no good ever comes from it.

We must not try to rename it or deny it when it is so deadly as to destroy us. We must always exercise our senses to be sensitive to everything that can infiltrate our homes and cause them to fail.

> "Set me as a seal upon thine heart, as a seal upon thine arm: for love is strong as death; jealousy is cruel as the grave: the coals thereof are coals of fire, which hath a most vehement flame" (Song of Solomon 8:6).

Restoring a Marriage Alone

Can a marriage be restored with only one partner making significant effort? Perhaps a better question to ask is, "Can only one person dedicated to Christ make a difference in the relationship?" The answer is yes. My experience has taught me that too often individuals seek excuses instead of answers. Many times neither person is willing to make an all-out effort to restore their home. A faltering home has little chance of success when neither party is willing to commit themselves to the Lord.

If just one of the two will commit to faithful church attendance, Bible reading, and dedication to God, the chances of restoration are dramatically enhanced. Imagine the impact of a dedicated spouse seeking God's highest and best for the relationship. Most marriages have been restored primarily by the influence of one party. Often, one of the spouses comes along reluctantly for counsel at the request of the other. Rarely do I have a couple come to my office in which both readily admit they need help.

Anyone willing to take the lead in seeking marriage restoration is to be commended. The commitment to restore a marriage alone requires a deep conviction that your decision will affect your life for years to come. Deciding to do right usually considers future consequences.

Your home is worth saving. Your decision affects four parents, probably your grandparents, almost certainly your children, very likely your grandchildren, and many friends and other relatives. Often divorce affects your work, your hobbies, and your daily routine. The decision involves money, companionship, possessions, and your future. Most people fail to realize the extent major marital decisions have on them and others.

Another consideration is that many will remarry after divorce. The statistics for second (or third) marriages are worse than those for first marriages. Failure to reconcile one marriage indicates the likelihood of failure at reconciling any marriage. The pain of a failed marriage often is repeated in a second which only compounds the problem. Seeking to restore your marriage through an unconditional commitment of agape love will yield great rewards.

There are always two sides to marriage problems, and fault is not always shared equally. Nevertheless it is always shared partially. When you make an unconditional commitment, you are saying, "I plan to fix my part of the problem." Amazingly when you repair your problems it often results in your partner searching their heart encouraging them to change. So often, holding on to those few little things hinders reconciliation. It is always difficult to love when you are not receiving love in return; it seems as if you are only doing it to obey God, uncertain if circumstances will ever change. What a blessing to know obedience to God can result in a wonderfully close relationship in the future.

Fasting and Prayer

Many times a wife or husband has sat in my office, assuring me she or he has done everything possible to save the marriage, but his/her spouse simply is not interested. Often problems have accumulated over a long time and the real cause has been clouded and confused. Being so close to the situation makes it very difficult to have the best perspective on your problems. A person who is truly open to the Lord's leading can find help through counsel, but sometimes life is so confused it's difficult to see the forest for the trees. Before I allow anyone to resign themselves that their situation is hopeless I always ask them if they have tried fasting and prayer. The look on their faces is amazing. They look at me as to say, I came to your for counsel and encouragement and all you can tell me is to fast and pray. Don't you realize I'm already suffering?

Many years ago an unconverted man visited one of our church services. After the service he requested to speak with me privately. As his story of woe unfolded my heart went out to this man. His wife had left him for another man and had taken their daughter with her. Often people come to me only seeking a remedy for their immediate problem, but in this case this man responded that he needed salvation and he was willing to commit his life to Christ regardless of whether or not his wife ever returned to him. This man was gloriously saved and quickly began to grow in the Lord. After only a few months his prodigal wife attended a service with him. I have never seen such a sad countenance. I considered this woman may never return to church again, but she did return and continued for a few months until finally she also received Christ as her Savior. This family was restored when there seemed to be no hope or possibility of restoration. I believe the key was this man's willingness to pray and depend completely upon God.

A lack of commitment to the marriage is the most dangerous threat possible to the longevity of any home.

Great problems require serious actions. God hears and answers prayer, but how serious have you been in your prayers? Serious prayer involves contrition, introspection, and dependence. Fasting is a lost virtue in today's churches. "Defraud ye not one the other, except it be with consent for a time, that ye may give yourselves to fasting and prayer; and come together again, that Satan tempt you not for your incontinency" (1 Corinthians 7:5). Several positives come as a result of fasting and prayer combined; however you will never know what God could have done if you never try. "You must not forget the God of Moses, Elijah and all the prophets is your God too. Now unto him that is able to do exceeding abundantly above all that we ask or think, according to the power that worketh in us" (Ephesians 3:20).

Why do marriages fail? Many problems can be cited: money problems, lack of communication, lack of intimacy, sexual problems, unfaithfulness, and apathy.

Many other problems could be cited as well, but if a couple is committed to the marriage, no matter what problem occurs, there will always be a resolve to find a solution. A lack of commitment to the marriage is the most dangerous threat possible to the longevity of any home. Believing it is God's will to work out problems in a marriage will result in a happy and successful home. Without commitment emotions will control decisions, and emotions can change from day to day. How much better it is to believe and trust God.

Gathering Lilies

Chapter Seven

Precious Memories

Periodically my wife and I would escape from all the pressures of the ministry and children by taking a brief retreat. These special times allowed us to be more intimate and personal. Such times of refreshment are important for every marriage. Life is busy, and taking these brief retreats helped us to keep our perspective. My wife especially looked forward to these events, which provided her a brief escape from work, raising children, serving in the ministry, and dealing with everyday life.

On one occasion I secretly planned a special getaway as a complete surprise to my wife. I found a babysitter for the children, packed the bags and planned the entire trip without my wife's knowledge. Janet usually doesn't like surprises, but she greatly appreciated the fact that I was willing to take the time to give her attention and to do something special for her.

Homes do not build themselves. I have never regretted taking valuable time to spend with my wife, but I have regretted periods that became too busy to spend the time we needed together. I have written many special notes to my wife and she has planned many special surprises for me. The first special occasion I can recall was two months after we were married. I returned home from work and school to some giant cookies my wife had prepared for me. They were shaped in the form of hearts and decorated in a special way. Not only were the cookies delicious, but the thought of my wife taking the time to do something special for me was a great blessing.

We have found the routine of life can become mundane and boring, and spicing it up with pleasant surprises has proved invaluable. Writing notes, baking special cookies or simply saying, "I love you" can be extremely important in creating the right atmosphere in your marriage. Over the years I have spent quite a sum of money on flowers, which have all since faded and died, but I do not consider them a bad investment. In fact my investment has created a sweet smell, like that of the lilies. The truth is that those special things have proven to be priceless. These special kindnesses are like the smell of lilies.

THE FRAGRANCE OF LILIES

The lily is one of the most fragrant and beautiful flowers in God's creation. Flowers are short lived, yet they add beauty and joy to life. Flowers have proven to be special gifts for many occasions and sometimes for no special occasion. Every wife loves to have a fresh bouquet of flowers to provide beauty and fragrance to her home

At the top of the pillars of the ancient Hebrew Temple lilies were inscribed, where only God could see them. This detail of the Temple was something no one could see except the Lord. Some things in life need to be done from the heart, with nothing expected in return. The Shulamite who is the maiden lover in the Song of Solomon, speaks several times of lilies in the small poetic book. Christ is considered to be the Lily of the Valley. "I am the rose of Sharon, and the lily of the valleys" (Song of Solomon 2:1). Every home needs some lilies!

We must never forget the beauty of our marriage.

I can picture a little freckled girl in a gingham dress, running through a field, picking flowers. She is carefree and enjoying the beautiful world around her. Chasing a butterfly or skipping rocks across a lake illustrate the carefree behavior that is common among youth. Every new marriage is special in God's eyes, and it is very much like the beauty of a small child, filled with joy and innocence. This beauty can easily be lost unless time is taken to recuperate from the pressures of life. We must never forget the beauty of our marriage.

The lilies are the intangible things of your marriage. Some people have referred to this as a spark, while others say they heard music playing. The way of a man with a maid is something very beautiful and special. The Song of Solomon should be read frequently by every husband and wife as a reminder of the special union they can enjoy together. This little book too often is forgotten or bypassed as insignificant. This beautiful story expresses the love of a young man for a young maid. The story is also a picture of Christ's love for us. The love between a man and a woman is as strong as death and never should be taken for granted.

Rekindling a Marriage

The unfortunate circumstances that can separate a married couple are a very real threat. As a newly married couple you may think your marriage could never be in jeopardy; however you must recognize that unless you build your home on the right foundation, you are likely to face trouble in the future. Marriage is a perfect illustration of this proverb: "An ounce of prevention is worth a pound of cure." A dull and unhappy home must be avoided at all costs.

Unfortunately, many couples will not heed their premarital counseling advice. Some never received any training concerning their marital union. But, troubles do come, and far more than often anticipated. Even if the joy has faded it's still possible to restore the spice and excitement of any marriage. No marriage is beyond hope if at least one of the parties is willing to follow Biblical teaching. However, a half-hearted effort to save a marriage will prove insufficient. Commitment to rebuild a marriage must be resolute. Loving your mate means you will not play emotional games of petty revenge or jealousy. Clinging, complaining, and temperamental displays of anger and moodiness never inspire love and will hinder restoration. Honesty and forgiveness both play an important role in restoring a fractured home; therefore it is vital that you search your own heart carefully so that you become completely transparent.

So how do you rekindle a dwindling fire? Rekindling the fire in your marriage begins with several little things. It is nearly impossible to start a fire with big logs, but if small twigs are first ignited, then larger ones can be ignited, which will light still larger ones. Ultimately you can ignite a great fire that is difficult to extinguish. Saying I love you, opening the car door, preparing a special meal, and many other small things can begin the spark needed. Trying to light the entire log is nearly impossible. Initiating a plan of several little things is a great place to start in re-igniting your relationship. At first these efforts may be ignored or rejected; however it is important to recognize this is the way to build your home and you are serious about it. Returning blessing for cursing can heap coals of conviction upon an offending party. Therefore if thine enemy hunger, feed him; if he thirst, give him drink: for in so doing thou shalt heap coals of fire on his head. (Romans 12:20)

Does Separation Help?

Choosing to separate for a period of time hinders the ability to show love and change. Seldom is it a good idea, and little good can come from such a decision. Situations of excessive physical violence or threats of harm to children need to be taken into consideration and may require leaving the home for a period of time to protect children. However most separations result from an unwillingness by either party to bend or change. Also, separation offers the opportunity for an unfaithful spouse to pursue another relationship with little restraint. Such an affair is difficult to compete with because it is without responsibility; it is a purely a physical and emotional situation. Staying together, though difficult, requires facing problems and responding to them. You must learn how to resolve your conflict rather than run from it.

Selfishness Is the Enemy of the Home

- "The wife hath not power of her own body, but the husband: and likewise also the husband hath not power of his own body, but the wife" (1 Corinthians 7:4).
- "What? know ye not that your body is the temple of the Holy Ghost which is in you, which ye have of God, and ye are not your own? For ye are bought with a price: therefore glorify God in your body, and in your spirit, which are God's" (1 Corinthians 6:19-20).

Acknowledge the good things your spouse does for you and return the favor.

Every Christian is purchased by Christ's blood, and we belong to Him. We no longer are to make decisions as we choose, but only in His perfect will. Not only do we belong to Christ, but through marriage we surrender our bodies and lives to our spouse. After marriage we must learn to make decisions that honor the Lord and our spouse. No one enjoys the company of a selfish individual, but everyone enjoys being with a generous person. No home is completely happy when either partner is selfish. Selfishness kills the joy of a marital relationship. We must all learn through the power of the Holy Spirit to be generous, kind, and loving—to display the fruit of the Spirit (Galatians 5). "Me first" never strengthens a home. Acknowledge the good things your spouse does for you and return the favor.

REJOICE WITH THE WIFE OF THY YOUTH

A newly married couple could be tempted to return back to their parents after a quarrel or when they need money or other such things. Wise couples will refuse this temptation, even if it means a temporary shortage of money or provisions. This fledgling couple must learn to depend upon each other. Their greatest need is to learn dependence and cleaving. When a problem occurs, who do you call? It should be your spouse, not your mother or father.

My youngest daughter is finishing college and it seems soon to be engaged. My wife and I have been in close contact with her boyfriend and his parents. Recently we discussed basic costs of setting up a home. I was asked what was expected for my future son-in-law, should he have his own car, an apartment, savings and if so how much? I responded, he didn't need any of those things, however if he married my daughter he would not live in my home and I would not give him a ride, so unless he wanted to live in a tent I suggested he buy a car and save some money. In other words they must leave home and make it on their own.

> "Drink waters out of thine own cistern, and running waters out of thine own well. Let thy fountains be dispersed abroad, and rivers of waters in the streets. Let them be only thine own, and not strang-

> ers' with thee. Let thy fountain be blessed: and rejoice with the wife of thy youth. Let her be as the loving hind and pleasant roe; let her breasts satisfy thee at all times; and be thou ravished always with her love" (Proverbs 5:15-19).

Water satisfies the most basic need in life. Fresh water in a dry land is wonderful refreshment. Just as a running stream of water in a desert blesses those who come into contact with it, so is a godly home a blessing to all who are touched by it. Consider the result of a young man and a young woman uniting in holy matrimony. From their love can come children who can one day become a blessing to the world. From the children can come yet another generation that honors the Lord and blesses those who come into contact with them. One marriage can influence the world through many offspring. Wherever that stream flows and touches another life, it is a testimony to the love and devotion of one couple. A godly marriage is a cistern from which flow blessings to a multitude of others. Solomon stressed the importance of Biblical love.

> "Set me as a seal upon thine heart, as a seal upon thine arm: for love is strong as death; jealousy is cruel as the grave: the coals thereof are coals of fire, which hath a most vehement flame. Many waters cannot quench love, neither can the floods drown it: if a man would give all the substance of his house for love, it would utterly be contemned" (Song of Solomon 8:6-7).

The first Sunday after I was married my new bride and I attended services at a church in a nearby town. The custom of this church was to ask visitors to stand and give their name. When they asked for visitors to stand, I stood and gave my name and my wife's name and then added, and we just were married two days ago. The people in the church all smiled and turned to look. There is something wonderful about marriage. It has the fragrance of a lily.

Dictionary.com. The American Heritage® Dictionary of the English Language, Fourth Edition. Houghton Mifflin Company, 2004. http://dictionary.reference.com/browse/cleave (accessed: February 21, 2007).

Section Two

CHILD TRAINING

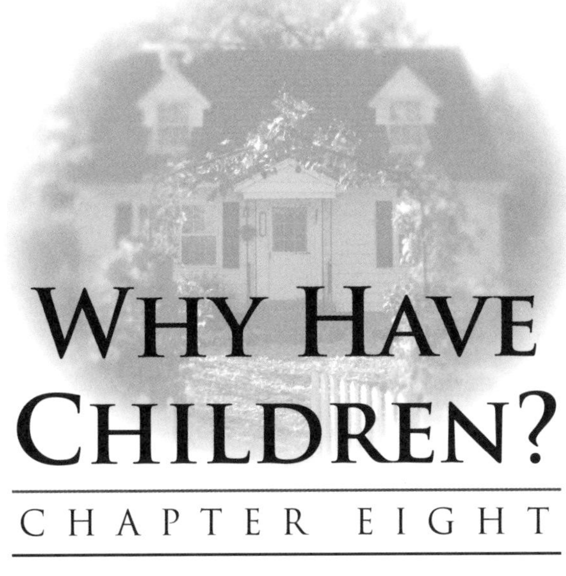

Why Have Children?

CHAPTER EIGHT

Precious Memories

Most parents suffer some emotional trauma when their children leave the nest. I have often said the only thing worse than your children leaving home is if they grow up and don't leave home. We must learn to enjoy our children while they are with us. It seems only yesterday we went to the hospital on an icy March day for Janet to give birth to our first child. We arrived at the hospital thinking this birth would require a few hours, only to have it develop into a three-day marathon. The birth of our first son was an unbelievable event, which gave us a new appreciation for life. Leaving the hospital with our own child seemed like a miracle—a fairy tale—and tomorrow we would wake up to realize it was all a dream.

But, we didn't have to wait for tomorrow because the little tyke woke up several times through the night to be fed. Our newborn baby soon taught us rearing children was a tremendous responsibility that required a great deal of attention. Now, as I reflect back on repeating the process three more times—and ultimately watching four children grow, mature, and leave home—I'm gratified that God gave them to us. I must admit there have been some difficult and traumatic—and expensive—times. Yet, now they are gone, and I miss those busy days. I miss the noise, the messes, and the responsibility. Your children eventually will grow up and leave your home. Enjoy the time together while you can. While your children are young it may seem as though the burden of their care will never end, but it will. Someday you will look back to those days and—if you raised them for the Lord—without regrets. My grandfather used to say; if you live long enough, someday you will be old. He was right. Enjoy the great task God has given you, because someday, if you live long enough, you will be old.

- "Whereas ye know not what shall be on the morrow. For what is your life? It is even a vapour, that appeareth for a little time, and then vanisheth away". (James 4:14).
- "Children's children are the crown of old men; and the glory of children are their fathers" (Proverbs 17:6).

Why Have Children?

Usually when I ask parents why they decided to have children they appear perplexed. Is it really our choice? I realize our culture largely believes in birth control, however everyone must agree children are a gift from God and no one can bear children unless God brings them into being. The emphasis of this chapter is not to discuss birth control, rather to influence the purpose to the children God grants you. The Bible exhorts man to be fruitful and multiply, therefore I believe God is well pleased when couples bear children. I differ with those who have the ability to have children and choose not to do so. Many people who have the honor of bringing life into this world have never considered the responsibility that comes with it bringing children into the world is a serious matter and must be done only with significant consideration.

Every child born is a living soul bound either for heaven or hell, and their life on earth will become a blessing or a curse.

I recall reading an article concerning a young couple choosing between having children and purchasing a new boat. Bringing life into the world should never be considered on the same level as a hobby. Every child born is a living soul bound either for heaven or hell, and their life on earth will become a blessing or a curse. The reason children are born should be as a result of two people's love for each other. God intended for two people to marry, bear children and bring honor to the Lord.

Before children arrive into a home their purpose may be given little thought, but years after the little ones arrive many parents have considered that very issue. The responsibility of bearing children should be understood prior to their arrival. The desire to have children is a normal and natural God-given instinct. In fact, the first couple, Adam and Eve, was commanded to be fruitful and multiply. Considering God's command to bring forth life we must recognize God has a purpose in couples bearing children. Though the natural instinct to fulfill God's command to be fruitful and multiply is compelling for almost all couples, the great responsibilities accompanying the birth of children can easily be underestimated. What seemed liked a good idea and perhaps "a fun new thing" can bring significant stress to a relationship. A once carefree life suddenly is burdened with responsibility. Whatever guided the decision to have children, the need of supernatural help is indisputable.

Past generations desired large families, partly because they benefited monetarily with every child born into their home. Boys helped dad with farming, gardening, tending to animals, and helping with the family business. Girls helped cook, care for the younger children, wash clothes, and care for the garden. While in the past each child helped provide for the family needs, today's children are not a monetary asset. Anyone who has children knows they are an expense and not a financial asset. With no financial incentive today to have children what purpose would there be?

The title of this chapter is why have children? The question could be rephrased by asking why children need parents. Parents can give their children purpose in life, thus a reason to have children is to guide them toward God's purpose. Rachel showed a great desire to have children when she said to Jacob, "Give me children or I die." Hannah not only desired children, but desired them for a specific purpose. She told the Lord that if He would enable her to have a son she would give him back to the Lord. All parents should learn this lesson of giving their children to the Lord. God gives children parents not only to be stewards of their welfare and training but to mold and form their lives with love and understanding. Realizing the tremendous responsibility of child training, parents must anticipate their children's developmental stages and help them prepare to meet life's daily challenges. Wise parents will help mold their child's character and purpose. As I observe parental behavior sometimes I wonder what led them to have children, and perhaps they wonder that same thing themselves. Parenting is serious business!

I recall a family with four adopted children. The kids rode the bus to Sunday school, and the parents attended the morning church service. Over time I detected a problem with the two teen children, which led me to initiate some counseling time with them. I learned the parents often told them they were stupid and said they wished the youngsters had never been born. The scars of this type of emotional damage can last a lifetime. Once children are born, it's too late to reconsider. You can't take them back to the hospital and drop them off.

The great love Jacob had for his sons Joseph and Benjamin illustrates the strong bond that develops between a child and his father. After being sold into slavery, Joseph became Egypt's acting ruler, under the pharaoh. During a great famine Joseph's brothers came to him to buy food for their family. Jacob's life was bound up in the life of his son Benjamin. In other words, Jacob was so mentally and emotionally tied to his son that any misfortune Benjamin might suffer would seem as if it was Jacob's personal misfortune. His son's life could not be separated from his own life. "Now therefore when I come to thy servant my father, and the lad be not with us; seeing that his life is bound up in the lad's life" (Genesis 44:30).

If parents can influence their children to love and desire secular interests, then as Christian parents we also should create in them a love and desire for spiritual interests. Joseph and Rose Kennedy had strong political aspirations, and they "groomed" all of their children for politics careers. If the Kennedy's could rear their children to love politics, then why can't Christian parents rear their children to love the Lord? The truth is, we can train our children to serve the Lord!

The ministry is the highest calling to which a young person can aspire, and parents should never fear surrendering their children to the Lord.

Parents who are involved and dedicated in serving the Lord seem to have the greatest success in raising children who are committed to serve the Lord. Children of pastors, deacons, custodians, bus workers, music directors, and other staff members often have great success in reproducing their godly commitment in their children. Christian servants who enjoy serving the Lord and include their children in the ministry will greatly enhance their children's desire to serve the Lord. The ministry is the highest calling to which a young person can aspire, and parents should never fear surrendering their children to the Lord. It is a worthy goal to help your children learn to love the Lord and be faithful to Him through the local church. If God should call your children to go to a foreign field, then rejoice with them in God's leading in their lives.

CHILDREN CAN BECOME A POWERFUL INFLUENCE

> "Except the LORD build the house, they labour in vain that build it: except the LORD keep the city, the watchman waketh but in vain. It is vain for you to rise up early, to sit up late, to eat the bread of sorrows: for so he giveth his beloved sleep. Lo, children are an heritage of the LORD: and the fruit of the womb is his reward. As arrows are in the hand of a mighty man; so are children of the youth. Happy is the man that hath his quiver full of them: they shall not be shamed, but they shall speak with the enemies in the gate." (Psalm 127:1-5).

As parents we must learn to rely completely on God. Anyone who considers himself an expert in child rearing either doesn't have children or is blind to their failures. God

---

Children serve no honoring purpose unless they have been aimed toward the right target.

---

can and must intervene for children to achieve their greatest potential. Psalm 127 explains the sad reality of faithless parents sitting up late and experiencing sorrow because their children are out of control. Children must be regarded as God's, and we are simply God's stewards to care for them. Children, then, are a heritage or an inheritance of the Lord for us to train in His service. When children are properly guided they become weapons, as an arrow mighty in battle, and a soldier to fight the enemy and thus provide spiritual peace. So children enable the name of God to be promoted and provide a hope for the future of a family, a community, or a country. Children who have been properly aimed or guided provide a sense of joy and blessing to their parents. Children serve no honoring purpose unless they have been aimed toward the right target.

"The rod and reproof give wisdom: but a child left to himself bringeth his mother to shame" (Proverbs 29:15). Children can become a detriment to society or a powerful influence for God. One of the largest companies in the world was built by teenagers. You are probably familiar with them, their name is McDonald's. If teens can build a huge corporation, imagine the power they possess to influence their world for Christ. Parents have the responsibility of directing their lives. I recall an evangelist who traveled to his meetings with his entire family in a motor home. When he arrived in our parking lot I welcomed him to our church and we discussed "preacher things," while I closely observed his teen boys as they opened our electrical panel and wired in their motor home, and then blocked and adjusted their home while their dad stood and talked with me. The dad never lifted a finger, because he had trained his boys to do the job. As a young father, that family made a strong impression on me. I knew this family was special. I watched and learned as much from the behavior of that man's children as I did from his sermons.

WHO IS THIS KID?

Upon asking a man how many children he had he responded three. Are they boys or girls? He responded I have one of each. The point he was making is not that children had no gender but that each one was unique. Understanding your child's personality can be a daunting challenge. I enjoy listening to parents wonder at their kids' personalities. Where did that come from? "That is my wife's son." Sometimes parents struggle to understand their child's personality when it differs from their own. Sometimes children seem to be "a chip off the old block," while at other times their behavior seems to be from some foreign source. Learning about and molding your children's personality, character, and talents is crucial to their development and maturity.

As I have mentioned previously, God blessed us with four children. I often say, "We had two boys, a girl, and Sarah." Our older daughter always has been feminine. But Sarah always played with our second son, Jonathan. Today Sarah is a beautiful young lady, preparing for marriage; but as a young lady her personality did not normally drive her to do feminine things. Our oldest son is extremely melancholy and very talented musically. Our second son, Jonathan, and his wife both love people and are outgoing. Our older daughter, Elizabeth, is more strong-willed than her dad and is determined to serve the Lord. Each one of our children offered special challenges and required wisdom from God to help them in the proper way.

Several fine books and articles have been written explaining the basic personality types. I would encourage every parent to read or conduct a serious search concerning this vital issue. Although the personality traits can be detailed to include more than 100 types, I prefer to simplify the descriptions with only four: *choleric*, *melancholy*, *phlegmatic* and *sanguine*. Although no two people are exactly the same, these four clear categories give a framework for understanding your child's personality. An even simpler approach is to recognize only two personality traits: task-oriented and people-oriented. Perceptive parents will notice, even while their children are still quite young, that they have certain personality traits. They may love animals or be fearful of them. Some children love music, while others may love sports. One child may enjoy solace , while another is always in the middle of the action. Children are not the same and need to be understood within the context of their God-given personality.

Children need not fulfill their parent's dreams of success; rather they need to fulfill God's best for their lives.

Recognizing your children's "bent" (character traits) will enable you to guide their development and skills more effectively. If a child loves music he can be encouraged to excel in this area. If she prefers sports, she should not be forced to play the violin. Expecting a child to excel in sports while he prefers science can create unrealistic expectations, hinder his well-being and produce a defeatist attitude. Children need not fulfill their parent's dreams of success; rather they need to fulfill God's best for their lives. Often a child can learn to participate in things in which he does not excel, but he should not be expected to excel in an area in which he has no strong interest. I loved basketball, and all of my children played, but two of them excelled at it, while the other two only enjoyed the experience. All of my children learned to play an instrument, but not all of them excelled in this area. By not pressuring them to perform at a high level of proficiency they enjoyed the camaraderie of participating in everything.

Commonly, people's personalities are divided into one of four different groups. The four groups are *sanguine*, *choleric*, *melancholy* and *phlegmatic*. The *sanguine* personality is a people person. He loves attention and is often the life of the party. For this personality type trivia is important, while details are not. The *choleric* is a person who has a serious temperament. He usually likes to be in charge and run the show. He can be very stubborn and is interested only in the facts. The *melancholy* personality is more thoughtful and internal. These folks are usually artistic or musically inclined and desire knowledge. They want to know why and how. Then there is the *phlegmatic* personality. They are usually shy and easy going and they like to be around people, but quietly so. No one is entirely one personality, but typically they are more dominant in one type.

A child's personality must not be confused with character. A personality is inherited and cannot be changed, while one's character should be in an ongoing process of change. A child's personality will be evident both positively and negatively. A person with a strong choleric personality always enjoys being in charge. The desire to be in charge is the bent of their personality, but if they have poor character no one will want to follow them. It is important to see the viability of your child's personality and develop his character to best complement his personality type. Scripture challenges parents to train their children in the way they should go, but understanding the way they should go is not a simple feat. The goal of every parent must be to help their children develop character and thus prove the best of their particular personality. We must not try to change them into something they are not or cannot be. "Train up a child in the way he should go: and when he is old, he will not depart from it" (Proverbs 22:6).

THE FAMILY NAME

The continuation of a family name is a motivation that has not been lost with the changing times. Families often take great pride in their name, and children bearing a family's name can be a source of great satisfaction. Recently I began researching the genealogy of my family. I found it to be enlightening and informative in ways I didn't expect. I quickly learned the importance of my family name. Names of parents and grandparents often are repeated as first or middle names in children and grandchildren. Mother's last names sometimes became children's first names and middle names. I traced several generations of my family and found James Townsley, James Enoch Townsley, James Enoch Camp Townsley, and James Joseph Alan Townsley, among others. Why do families name their children after their parents and grandparents? A family's name represents their reputation to their friends and neighbors. Disgracing the family name brings grief to all the family. The sole purpose of children is not merely to continue the family name, but to maintain it with a good and honorable reputation.

As a young boy my grandfather showed me a letter from his neighbor. The letter expressed gratitude toward my grandfather as being a model neighbor. He had volunteered in time of need and had proven himself to be a kind and considerate person. I can't remember everything in the letter, but I do recall the importance my grandfather placed upon this matter. His example created a high expectation for me. If a man loses his reputation he has suffered a great loss. "A good name is rather to be chosen than great riches, and loving favour rather than silver and gold" (Proverbs 22:1).

THE BIBLICAL REASONS TO HAVE CHILDREN

1. To bring them to salvation.
   - "Who will have all men to be saved, and to come unto the knowledge of the truth" (1 Timothy 2:4).
   - "The Lord is not slack concerning his promise, as some men count slackness; but is longsuffering to us-ward, not willing that any should perish, but that all should come to repentance" (2 Peter 3:9)
2. To leave an inheritance.
3. To continue a godly heritage.
   - "Lo, children are an heritage of the LORD: and the fruit of the womb is his reward" (Psalm 127:3).
4. To fulfill God's command to be fruitful and multiply.
   - "The children of thy servants shall continue, and their seed shall be established before thee" (Psalm 102:28).

- "Children's children are the crown of old men; and the glory of children are their fathers" (Proverbs 17:6).
- "If a man beget an hundred children, and live many years, so that the days of his years be many, and his soul be not filled with good, and also that he have no burial; I say, that an untimely birth is better than he" (Ecclesiastes 6:3).

GOALS

Parents must have goals for their children and a plan to achieve these goals. Children do not achieve success alone. God has given them to us to guide them and encourage them. What goals do you have for your children? Whatever your goals may be, they will require you to communicate with your children and give them the support and encouragement needed to achieve them. Everyone needs goals. Aim at nothing and you are bound to hit it.

Worldly parents may choose to direct their children toward secular goals, such as a high-paying job, purchasing a nice home, buying a new car, or achieving prominence in the community. Christian families should have more lofty expectations of their children. Discovering and doing God's will is the highest goal possible for a believer.

Learning the fear of the Lord is a foundational element of a Christian's life. Proverbs 1:7 expresses the importance of fearing God. "The fear of the LORD is the beginning of knowledge: but fools despise wisdom and instruction." Learning to love the Lord is another basic tenet of Christianity.

The shema (Deuteronomy 6:4) was given to Jewish families to teach their children, and it remains a foundational truth for every believer.

> "Hear, O Israel: The LORD our God is one LORD: And thou shalt love the LORD thy God with all thine heart, and with all thy soul, and with all thy might. And these words, which I command thee this day, shall be in thine heart: And thou shalt teach them diligently unto thy children, and shalt talk of them when thou sittest in thine house, and when thou walkest by the way, and when thou liest down, and when thou risest up" (Deuteronomy 6:4-7).

> "And if it seem evil unto you to serve the LORD, choose you this day whom ye will serve; whether the gods which your fathers served that were on the other side of the flood, or the gods of the Amorites, in whose land ye dwell: but as for me and my house, we will serve the LORD" (Joshua 24:15).

Following leadership is another important aspect of the Christian life that must be taught. Submitting to authority and learning to adhere to instruction is a vital element in serving the Lord. From the earliest age children must learn to respond to their parents' commands and advice. Failure to do so will lead to certain destruction. "My son, hear the instruction of thy father, and forsake not the law of thy mother: For they shall be an ornament of grace unto thy head, and chains about thy neck" (Proverbs 1:8, 9).

Another important character trait that must be developed in the life of Christian young people is learning to associate with the right people. Sometimes it becomes necessary to stand alone, but often the choice is standing against the ungodly and with the righteous. "Blessed is the man that walketh not in the counsel of the ungodly, nor standeth in the way of sinners, nor sitteth in the seat of the scornful" (Psalm 1:1).

Besides those virtues previously mentioned, every child must learn dependability, honesty, kindness, humility, temperance, and diligence. Ask yourself what traits you believe should be exemplified in your children and then ask yourself how you will instill these qualities in them. The method of teaching these traits is twofold: 1) *Modeling* these qualities before them in your life and 2) *teaching* them daily as opportunities avail themselves. Unrealistic goals create frustration and discouragement, but teach your children to do their best and let them know their best is good enough. Be proud of them for putting forth their best effort. Whether it is in education, sports, or Christian service, commend them for doing their best.

We must remember that children are like arrows that need to be aimed and directed toward a target. Parents are given approximately twenty years to directly influence their children's character, and as soon as they are born the clock begins ticking. Don't delay; get started directing them toward godly goals immediately.

Admonishing Children

Chapter Nine

Precious Memories

I was my mother's parents' only grandson. Mom's parents had three daughters, four granddaughters, and one grandson, me. I referred to my grandfather as *Dad* and my grandmother as *Mom.* I was the son they had long desired, and there is no doubt I received special treatment because of it. My sister was special because she was the first grandchild, but being the only son and grandson especially benefited me.

As a young child I assumed every child received the same special treatment as I received. My grandfather allowed me to help in the hay field while I was still very young. Once he needed someone to steer the truck while they loaded it with hay bails. He started the truck forward in its lowest gear and stood me on the seat to steer the truck. After a short time I decided the truck wasn't going fast enough so to gain more speed I climbed down from the seat and pushed on the accelerator with my hand. My grandfather ran to see what had happened and when he found me on the truck's floor, trying to accelerate, he had a good laugh.

My childhood was greatly influenced by my family. I cannot change my past, even if I desired to do so. As I reflect on my childhood I am eternally grateful for many aspects of it. Though I was very fortunate to have a good family, it was not perfect. Since I can't change my past, I must accept it. My experiences form who I am, whether good or bad. I choose to build on my good experiences.

I imagine every person would change some things if they could, but it is important to realize our past is an accumulation of good and bad, and we may learn from both. Learning to accept who we are and recognize that we are sinners helps us form a proper perspective for the future. The things I cannot change I must accept, and the things I can change, by God's grace, I will. "And we know that all things work together for good to them that love God, to them who are the called according to his purpose" (Romans 8:28).

TEACHING CHILDREN ABOUT CHURCH

It was early April in Connecticut when my wife and I arrived to start a new church. We had made arrangements to stay with a family in a neighboring town until we found an apartment to rent. Upon entering their home the father showed me pictures of his children and family. His next action really surprised me; he removed a picture from his mantle to proudly reveal a picture of his pastor. He wanted me to know how much he loved his pastor. His family all loved their pastor and his wife. That experience has stayed with me all these years. I was not surprised to see all of his children grow up to faithfully serve the Lord. They learned to love their church and their pastor through their parents' encouragement. When children learn to respect their pastor they learn to respect God. Parents who criticize their pastor damage their children

---

Belonging to a good church is important for children, because it will form a strong worldview that will influence their entire future.

---

by destroying a main source of encouragement. Upholding the office of the pastor and praying for him will give children a desire to please those in authority and especially to please the Lord.

Belonging to a good church is important for children, because it will form a strong worldview that will influence their entire future. Wasting time in a dead church is a fatal mistake. Likewise, choosing a church where your children find the most enjoyment is a gross error. Sometimes a small mission church will be a great learning center for children. Other times a church may be larger and boast many ministries and activities. If you need to find a good church, pray for God to lead your family to the place of His choosing. The church with the most activities and the most children the age or yours may cause them to be happy, but not necessarily to be dedicated. Most people would be better served to learn to love the church they presently attend. If a church is not friendly, then help to change it rather than complain. Teach your children to be friendly, to serve and not be served, teach them to be a blessing rather than to receive a blessing. Teach them to listen to the preaching and apply the messages to their life. The attitude of the parents toward their church and pastor will most certainly influence the attitude of the children.

Children should not hinder parents from serving the Lord; rather they should enhance their service. Provided there are no complications, parents should bring their newborns to church with them. As soon as possible, utilize the church nursery. Leaving your children in the church nursery is your first opportunity to teach them to trust you to return for them. It also allows you and others to listen to the sermon and to continue in your area of service. I have observed parents who constantly allowed their children to hinder their involvement in church. Parents cannot waste years waiting for their children to grow up before they serve the Lord. A family that has four children over a period of ten years could become very backslidden by the time their last child is in school. God did not intend parents to produce offspring who keep them from serving Him, rather He intends children to be taught to serve the Lord by their parents' faithfulness.

Our church was a tightly knit family while our children were young. Consequently, holding the preacher's children was a special privilege nursery workers relished. The problem was that on Monday our children expected the same service they received on Sunday. Every Monday our children experienced withdrawal from lavish treatment. Mondays were always our children's worst day of the week, but it never hindered us from continuing the same pattern, week after week.

I was born into a family of farmers. I had no choice in the matter, I was a farmer and my sister was a farmer. I was a one-year-old farmer, later a two-year-old farmer, and eventually I was a teenage farmer. Farming was a family "calling" to which I can't recall ever being given an option. Children born to Christian parents must realize their family is a Christian family and they must act accordingly. No one need ask, "Are we going to church." Church attendance should already be settled. From an early age children must learn faithful church attendance. Keeping children home during evening church meetings teaches children they have an option as to church attendance. If children have an early bedtime during school

Learning to appreciate the preaching and the music during the church meeting will provide lasting impressions, even for the smallest worshippers.

nights, encourage them to take a nap before the service. I recall a mother who kept her child home for three years before she or her son attended church. Children need to learn faithfulness and to enjoy attending church.

Children must learn how to sit quietly and respectfully in church at an early age. Playing games and having fun is not the purpose of a church service. While sitting with their parents they learn to enjoy the service, not just come to church to have fun. Teaching a young child to sit quietly may require a few weeks of sitting in the back of the auditorium and periodically taking them out to be disciplined. But eventually they will learn to sit properly.

Playing with toys and turning and looking at others must not be tolerated. Going to the restroom during the service should not happen. Parents must remind their children to go before the service begins, because when the service starts it will be too late. To avoid distractions, those who leave a service due to illness should sit in the back when they return. Proper church etiquette must be taught at an early age.

Many positive things can be learned in the service. Children can learn to take notes, and after the service they can be questioned about what they learned. Children learn the importance of sitting respectfully during the service. Participating in the singing will teach children music that honors the Lord. Learning to appreciate the preaching and the music during the church meeting will provide lasting impressions, even for the smallest worshippers. The fear of God and love for the Lord can be learned during the early years. Children can learn the importance of giving. Initially, money can be provided for them to give to the Lord. Parents should set the example. The Bible teaches it is more blessed to give than to receive. Children can participate in prayer; they can respond to the invitation to the message and many other aspects of worship. Work days and special activities offer opportunities for children to serve with their parents. Serving the Lord should be a family thing. Children should learn to sit with their family, especially while they are young. Children sitting with their friends usually get into trouble. Sitting with friends should only be allowed if it is in front of their parents, in clear view.

While our children were small they learned to help prepare the auditorium for Sunday. They moved chairs, adjusted hymnbooks, cleaned the floor, and set up classrooms. As soon as they could drag a chair to a spot they learned to be a helper.

I believe because they started at such a young age they even learned to enjoy doing it. Encourage your children to love their church.

YOUR CHILDREN'S SALVATION

Leading your children to trust Christ as their personal Savior must be the first and most important priority among your parental duties. Our Lord has a special love for children, and parents must realize the great responsibility in teaching

Leading your children to trust Christ as their personal Savior must be the first and most important priority among your parental duties.

them the message of salvation. It is a wonderful privilege to lead your children to faith in Christ and observe their continual growth in the Lord. Though your family name may be held in the highest regard, it will not provide a new name in heaven. Every person must make their own decision to trust Christ. The Holy Spirit must convict a soul of his lost condition and of the sufficiency of Christ's atonement, then that person may call upon the Savior to create in him a new heart.

- "But as many as received him, to them gave he power to become the sons of God, even to them that believe on his name: Which were born, not of blood, nor of the will of the flesh, nor of the will of man, but of God" (John 1:12, 13).

Every man must personally give account of his own life. Like any other man, every child must face the truth that they are lost and condemned.

- "He that believeth on him is not condemned: but he that believeth not is condemned already, because he hath not believed in the name of the only begotten Son of God" (John 3:18).

From the time of a child's birth, parents must commence praying for their salvation. The Bible must be read and explained. Bible stories and lessons must be learned. Character must be taught and the necessity of salvation must be emphasized. However, all the teaching and exhortation is not sufficient unless the child chooses to be saved. Pray daily for the conversion of your children.

Often parents come to me and suggest their young child is ready to be saved. I recall one such incident in which the parents assured me their child understood all that was necessary to be saved, but they wanted me to speak to their child and give them my evaluation of her spiritual state. I am always cautious when a child is very young, for I know they could be blinded to their lost condition for years to come if they make a false profession of faith. The parents remained with me as I questioned their daughter. I asked her, "What do you believe a person needs to do in order to go to heaven?" She gave a good Baptist answer, "You need to be saved." Then I asked her what else a person needed to do in order to get to heaven and she responded, "Be baptized." At this point her parents realized she didn't give the correct answer. Then I asked, "Is there anything else a person must do in order to get to heaven?" She responded, "Live a good life." This little girl did not yet understand the matter of faith in the finished work of Christ. In addition, she had not yet been convinced of salvation by grace alone, apart from works. By asking the right questions, I helped the parents realize their daughter was not yet prepared. I finished our session by encouraging this girl to continue to pray that God would reveal to her the clear plan of salvation, and as soon as she understood it she could call on the Lord to be saved. Later this lttle girl did trust Christ as her Savior and was gloriously saved.

Teaching the importance of the new birth is crucial. However, asking children to claim salvation prematurely can be a mistake. Once children make that decision they tend to push it to the back of their mind. Teaching and challenging children concerning the matter of salvation is important, but caution should be exercised to avoid "drawing the net" prematurely.

Two spiritual ingredients must be present in order for your children to make a decision for salvation. 1) *They must have the knowledge of salvation.* No one can be saved without understanding some very basic foundational truths. I realize of course that it is not necessary to understand every Christian doctrine, but the doctrines of salvation are imperative to understand. No man can be saved if he doesn't understand that all humans are lost sinners. Apart from Christ, our sin has condemned us, and without regeneration we are doomed to an eternal hell. Also, they must understand that Christ's sacrifice on Calvary was sufficient to pay the penalty for all of their sin. As the song writer well penned, "Jesus paid it all."

In addition, each child must make his own decision to receive Christ by repenting from his sin and placing his faith in the Savior's death on the cross at Calvary. 2) *The Holy Spirit must draw a person to salvation or he cannot be saved.* Without the Holy Spirit's conviction a person can understand the gospel message. To be saved, the Holy Spirit must move on one's heart to receive Christ as Savior. "No man can come to me, except the Father which hath sent me draw him: and I will raise him up at the last day" (John 6:44).

INVESTING IN THE LIVES OF YOUR CHILDREN

All our children were born in a local hospital and delivered by a trained medical professional. The hospital and doctor both sent us a hefty bill. Upon leaving the hospital the costs kept coming. Clothes and food as well as many other necessary baby items were needed. None of our babies came with an endowment or financial help. After starting school they required money for tuition, new clothes, food, doctors, and many items too numerous to mention. Each year the cost of having children became greater. Costs for such things as sports, music lessons, hunting, fishing, bicycles, skateboards, skates, golf, and skiing, along with several other hobbies and activities, only increased with their age. We gave extensive time to coach, attend games, drive to music lessons, take hunting and fishing trips, and go on vacations, as well as daily routines, all of which involved hundreds of hours of time. During their childhood they contributed nothing substantial to our financial status while costing us thousands of dollars.

If rearing children were viewed only as a financial decision, no one would ever have children. The high cost of raising a family would be viewed as a waste of time and money. However, I see our children as an investment in the future. Developing character requires time and money, but the return is priceless. I receive a personal satisfaction from knowing all my children are now serving the Lord. The expense was worth every penny and every minute. Anything of great value has a

---

Reading good books that teach character and Christian principles is invaluable in the early childhood years.

---

great cost. Nothing of substance comes without a price. But the time spent training my children was a great investment. There were the times of teaching them to clean the church, mow the church lawn, do landscaping, build buildings, go on visitations, and numerous other ministries that required valuable training time. Sometimes my children complained, as children tend to do, and I would respond, "You should be thankful, you are receiving free training, while most people are required to pay for this type of education." They knew it was coming and would just roll their eyes. But, today if you would ask them about their free training, you'd find they are extremely grateful for all those lessons they learned.

PRACTICAL WAYS TO ADMONISH YOUR CHILDREN

Read to your children. Reading good books that teach character and Christian principles is invaluable in the early childhood years. Children enjoy stories and learn basic lessons from them. Reading Bible stories is a very important habit for young minds, and early on daily Bible reading must become a staple in the home. We will be the same tomorrow as we are today, except for the books we read and the people we meet. Music also is a powerful influence on individuals and society. Providing good music during the early childhood years develops a taste for the right kind of music. Music is a powerful medium that can generate lofty thoughts of God or a rebellious spirit. The music children learn at an early age will provide an appreciation for godly music that will remain with them for a long time.

Hugs and kisses provide a sense of safety and security and are good reasons to hold and touch your children. Man is made in such a way that caresses are needful. Abundant love and affection should be displayed, particularly while children are young. Well-adjusted children have been given much love and affection. Learn to be generous with caresses to your little ones. I remember a special occasion when my last daughter was nearing the end of her childhood years. She walked into the living room and I suddenly realized how old she was becoming so I said to her, "Come sit on daddy's lap; I want to hold you for awhile." That may have been the last occasion I had to hold her on my lap. At the time she didn't understand why I wanted to hold her, but I knew soon she would be too old to sit on my lap. We must cherish the moments while we can. Children who receive proper attention from their parents while they are young will avoid the danger of seeking that love from the wrong source later in life.

Every child has an inclination toward some skill, and parents should help them to learn it. Discover your children's inclinations. Do they enjoy music? Perhaps they are more mechanically inclined. Maybe they enjoy flowers or birds. Children have an inclination toward something more than television and electronic games. Find the activities your children seem to respond to and endeavor to help them develop the skills for those activities. Provide the opportunity and means for them to be involved, to learn and gain confidence through them. Television is a powerful source of entertainment and information; however its bad side (sex and violence) is equally well documented. Though the social ills of television should concern parents, the time wasted—time that could have been used to develop character and skill—should be as great a concern. I know several families that do not own a TV, and I believe they are better for it. Depending on whose poll you read, Americans watch roughly twenty-five hours of television per week. Imagine if some of that time were spent teaching and encouraging your children.

Give them responsibility. Caring for a pet, cleaning their room, and taking out the trash are basic tasks every child must learn. However, wise parents can develop other responsibilities. Helping in the care and upkeep of the home can gradually be taught. Cooking, sewing, cleaning the car, and changing the car's oil are only a few suggestions. My children claim I am an expert at finding things for them to do. However, they all admit today they are capable of performing many tasks their peers cannot do. Helping neighbors and public service should be a part of every young person's life. Writing thank-you notes should be encouraged whenever necessary. Children should be taught to send thank-you notes to those who give them Christmas and birthday presents.

Recognize your children's age capabilities. Children are often capable of tasks earlier than most parents recognize. However, children must not be held accountable for more than they are capable of doing. Allow them to be children, and don't make them become adults prematurely. Allow them

---

I strongly believe parents must become interested in their children's interests.

---

to make mistakes, from which they can learn. Small children may break the vase left on the coffee table, so why not leave an unbreakable vase there while they're learning not to touch it. Taking away the vase would remove the opportunity to train them to do right. Removing the struggle may eliminate the opportunity to teach and admonish them. I would much rather a child struggle with the command to restrain from touching a vase than fail and struggle later in life with a much more important challenge. When you see them doing well, let them know. Take advantage of the good behavior to create a sense of high expectation. Seek opportunities to admonish your children and use the daily opportunities provided to do so.

I have been asked several times, what is the key to child training? Although there is no single answer, I strongly believe parents must become interested in their children's interests. Lovingly considering each child's desires, fears and triumphs will build trust and respect for a lifetime. Proving your love by caring for their needs will build a relationship that can influence your children to follow the Lord. Parents must recognize this great opportunity available to them and utilize it to its fullest extent. Take the time to learn the thoughts and cares of the little ones to whom God has entrusted you. If you don't express your concern for their physical needs, how can they understand your concern for their spiritual needs?

What determines a child's future? Every young person is a result of their physical make-up, as well as influence from their parents, friends, books, media, life experiences and, most importantly, from God. Therefore wise parents will seek to provide all the best influences to help their children become the best Christians they can be.

NURTURING THE HEART

CHAPTER TEN

PRECIOUS MEMORIES

Being firstborn is akin to being a guinea pig. Our first child was no exception. It soon became apparent that our first child, David, was strong willed. At first we thought there was no hope for him to learn to obey. Much of our daily energy was exerted in trying to keep ahead of his activity. It seemed every day he presented new challenges. My wife and I realized that because we were bigger than he was we could force him to obey, but our real desire was for him to respond from his heart.

I tried implementing the standard strategy of counting to three, hoping the deadline would impress upon this young rebel the need to respond immediately. Eventually he did learn to respond, but it was always just after I reached the number three. David, had learned to disobey for two counts before he obeyed once. After considerable thought I determined to employ a new method. My wife and I sat down with our son and explained that he must respond immediately or he would be disciplined. We further explained that we would now count to one and he must respond when we reached that number. The first time we tried this new technique I could see the wheels turning in his head. He was uncertain just how to adjust to this immediate deadline. He soon learned to obey immediately and we continued to employ this tactic with our other children.

I recall a humorous experience one day while shopping in the grocery store. David was doing something unacceptable so I said, "I'm counting to one and you better stop before I get to one." A grocery clerk overheard our conversation and remarked, "That poor boy doesn't have a chance. My parents always gave me to the count of three." Of course not giving him a chance to disobey was exactly our intention. "And, ye fathers, provoke not your children to wrath: but bring them up in the nurture and admonition of the Lord" (Ephesians 6:4).

TEACH THEM TO RESPOND TO YOUR AUTHORITY

Wise parents must learn to submit themselves to God as the ultimate authority. Bossing children and telling them to do as you say may result in outward compliance while rebellion begins to boil beneath the surface. Parents who are submissive to God can explain to their children they need God's help and they intend to follow His leading. Children are much more apt to become submissive when parents exemplify that same spirit in their lives. Respect for authority is not only taught, it is also caught. Children can learn to appreciate and love those in authority over them. Forced compliance works while they are young, but teaching them to obey from the heart lasts a lifetime.

Respect for all authority must be taught. We need to teach children to esteem police officers, government officials, Sunday school teachers, pastors, youth leaders, and all others who may be authority figures in their life. Allowing a child to argue with a teacher, principal, or youth leader ultimately will result in an openly rebellious young person.

My elementary school was in a small country setting in, believe it or not, Pleasantville, Indiana. As a young student

---

We must learn to respect and appreciate those who stand before us.

---

attending a public school I cannot recall any parent questioning a teacher's decision concerning their child. If a child came home and reported being punished in school the parents always sided with the authority. Parents never considered complaining to the principal. Today's culture unfortunately has changed, and now it is common for parents to defend their children against the school's authority. Constantly questioning God-given authority will certainly influence children to do the same. We must learn to respect and appreciate those who stand before us.

My children all attended a Christian school, where for a time I was the principal. I remember on one occasion my children returned home from school to announce a policy change. As the principal I was responsible for all policies and initiated changes as they were necessary. However, in this situation my children somehow received the wrong message. I knew the teacher was wrong and the message my children were telling me was wrong, but I never let them know the teacher had made a mistake. I waited until the next day and explained the problem to the teacher, and I allowed the teacher to explain the truth to my children. I could have destroyed that teacher's reputation if I had said what I knew to be true. My children would have returned to school the next day and promptly informed their teacher she was wrong, but it was not my children' place to do so. I am grateful God gave me the grace to remain quiet until I could follow the proper channels of authority to correct the problem.

Children must develop a heart to obey all God-given authority; failure to do so will result in children with an arrogant, unteachable spirit. Your ultimate goal should not be forcing them to comply, but rather teaching them the blessing of submitting their will to those God has placed in authority. Children must learn self-control because *one day they will be required to control themselves* and make their own decisions. Nurturing your child's heart involves more than telling him how to act or what to think, it involves investing your time and communicating truth, while warning him of potential dangers. As children observe the righteous behavior of their parents their thinking and lifestyle will be molded accordingly.

Memorizing Scripture is a very profitable exercise for children, but memorization alone is not enough. Scripture can stay with a person all of their life; however, memorizing Scripture must be accompanied with lessons about how to live the truth that is taught. Memorization alone will have no effect on behavior unless it is taken to heart. The Bible must be explained, reiterated, and applied to real-life situations. All of this teaching should be heartfelt by the teachers and exemplified in our lives.

THE HEART OF THE MATTER IS THE MATTER OF THE HEART

> "For from within, out of the heart of men, proceed evil thoughts, adulteries, fornications, murders, Thefts, covetousness, wickedness, deceit, lasciviousness, an evil eye, blasphemy, pride, foolishness: All these evil things come from within, and defile the man." (Mark 7:21-23)

Action comes from the heart. Not all outward action can be judged by external appearance, as is illustrated by David's life. Saul (David's predecessor as king) was a handsome and strong man, but he was not a good leader. God rejected King Saul and eventually anointed David, a man "after His own heart." When Samuel came to Jesse and said he would anoint one of his sons as King, Jesse was certain it would be his oldest son, Eliab. However, God could see David's heart, so He had Samuel anoint David, not Eliab to be Saul's successor. "But the LORD said unto Samuel, Look not on his countenance, or on the height of his stature; because I have refused him: for the LORD seeth not as man seeth; for man looketh on the outward appearance, but the LORD looketh on the heart" (1 Samuel 16:7).

Every parent truly concerned with the godly maturity of their children must recognize the need to nurture their heart.

One's environment affects behavior, but a person with a good heart can thrive in a bad environment. Consider Daniel and his three Hebrew friends. They were in a foreign, pagan country, yet they stood firm on their convictions. The three young men were thrown into a fiery furnace because they wouldn't bow to the King's image. Daniel illustrates this truth again

Parents must make the effort to influence their children at the heart level and not be satisfied merely with outward compliance.

when, because he continued to pray to God in spite of the new decree to pray only to the emperor, he was thrown into a den of lions. Also consider Samuel who as a child was given to serve in Eli's house. Eli's sons were hypocrites, yet in the same environment Samuel became God's choice servant. These godly young men learned to guard their heart. "Keep thy heart with all diligence; for out of it are the issues of life" (Proverbs 4:23).

A Christian school is no substitute for a right heart. Home schooling can protect children from society's many evil influences, but a good environment without a good heart will not produce godliness. Parents must make the effort to influence their children at the heart level and not be satisfied merely with outward compliance. It is within your control to determine the influences to which you will subject your children. Learning your children's inclinations and how they respond to different situations is an ongoing process during their developmental years. Make a habit of studying their behavior, and never allow yourself to be clouded by their mistakes. Denying their sins and shortcomings hinders your guidance to mold their behavior according to God's direction.

A little boy sat at the family dinner table when he abruptly stood to his feet to rudely reach across the table for his food. The father sternly warned his son to sit down immediately, to which the child responded, "I will sit down, but in my heart I am still standing." This experience reveals the importance of teaching heart compliance along with outward conformity. "Not with eyeservice, as menpleasers; but as the servants of Christ, doing the will of God from the heart" (Ephesians 6:6).

CONSIDER YOUR CHILD'S PERSONALITY

Understanding your children requires flexibility in your thinking. Every child has a unique personality. A child whose personality conflicts with his parents' personality requires special understanding. A melancholy mother and choleric daughter may find it difficult to understand one another—and that can cause frustration. A melancholy person likes lengthy explanations and often views situations in black and white, or right or wrong. A choleric personality looks at the bottom line and is usually interested in the basic facts that determine the final result. Also a choleric child enjoys a challenge, so when a mother commands her choleric daughter to obey, a battle may be in store. A wise mother will understand how to challenge her daughter properly. Instead of saying, "You must do the dishes," try asking her whether she would prefer to do the dishes or sweep the floor. This gives an element of control back to the daughter, and she will feel empowered to choose. I have witnessed this many times, and it is amazing how much work a child with this personality can accomplish if challenged in the right way.

Learn how to motivate your children. You don't have to be a psychologist to understand them, but you do have to spend time with them and pray for wisdom. A melancholy child needs clear explanations. Often the explanation is more important than the result. A phlegmatic child needs encouragement and patience, while a sanguine child needs friends and fun. Understanding their personality will help you bring out the best character in them. You can't change their personality, but you can influence their character, and it is important to know the difference. "I will praise thee; for I am fearfully and wonderfully made: marvellous are thy works; and that my soul knoweth right well" (Psalm 139:14).

The application of God's Word will help to discern and develop a child's heart. Realizing the battles of child rearing are fought in that little compartment known as the heart, nurturing and developing the heart should be the primary goal of every parent. True success in childrearing will reach a child's heart. "For the word of God is quick, and powerful, and sharper than any twoedged sword, piercing even to the dividing asunder of soul and spirit, and of the joints and marrow, and is a discerner of the thoughts and intents of the heart" (Hebrews 4:12).

Children look for significance in life. Parents must provide importance to their children by showing them love, affection, and discipline. When a child finds relationships that bring him significance he often cannot discern whether they are good or bad. Parents who bring significance to a child will provide his needs at home so that he need not find it in the world. Teenage fads invariably come and go as young people seek significance among their peers. Provide for their needs at home and they will not need to look elsewhere.

Encouragement is a powerful tool.

Someone once told me, "Everybody is having a hard time; therefore we should provide encouragement to everyone." That statement is not far from reality. Encouragement is a powerful tool. With encouragement your children can accomplish great things. Do your best to provide opportunities for them to struggle *and excel.* During the 1984 Los Angeles Olympics the women's marathon provided a breathtaking experience as Gabrielle Andersen-Scheiss staggered into the stadium, suffering from heat exhaustion. Spectators and viewers alike watched in amazement, uncertain what would happen next. Her coach wasn't certain if he should tell her to quit or encourage her to finish. Finally he decided to encourage her to finish the race. Through her coach's encouragement she completed the final lap in over five minutes. Finally she fell across the finish line. Encouragement is a powerful motivator, and your encouragement can motivate your children to great heights.

Global Protectionism

> "Love not the world, neither the things that are in the world. If any man love the world, the love of

> the Father is not in him. For all that is in the world, the lust of the flesh, and the lust of the eyes, and the pride of life, is not of the Father, but is of the world. And the world passeth away, and the lust thereof: but he that doeth the will of God abideth for ever." (1 John 2:15-17)

Global protectionism is a relatively new term that refers to world economics, with two primary viewpoints. One position states that trading with other countries is not needed for our economy to thrive. The ideal of global protectionism is to never import or export goods and services but to be self-sustaining as a country. Often protectionists fear losing their job to someone in a third-world nation, and that fear drives men to withdraw from the world scene and depend entirely upon this nation for everything. The opposing view promotes free trade and world competition as good for our country. The belief is that the open market will produce more competition and ultimately greater wealth for the country. This section is not about global economics, but it has some similarities to it. Every Christian must beware of the evils of the world. Don Fortner warns us sternly of the world's evil:

> Worldliness is not easily observed.
> It is not to be measured by the style of our clothes,
> the means of innocent relaxation and entertainment,
> or the place of our residence.
>
> Worldliness is the love of the world, the atmosphere of greed, the spirit of ambition, the passion for plea-

> sure and self gratification which consumes the hearts, lives, thoughts, and deeds of lost souls.

While we are warned of the evil in the world, we also are admonished to reach the world. The Bible teaches we are in the world, but we are not be "of the world." God loved the world so much that He gave His only begotten son so that men could be saved. We must love those in the world and yet we are commanded not to love the things of the world. To reconcile these apparent contradictions we must separate souls from the wicked world system. Christians are to love lost souls. Every Christian must admit that only by God's grace are we saved. No man, woman, or child deserves God's grace. Remember that God loved us when we were unlovely sinners (Romans 5:8). The key to nurturing is finding the balance of loving a lost world and separating from the evil in it. As the Bible teaches, we are to be in the world but not of the world.

Worldliness is condemned in Scripture. Wise parents must recognize that children can be influenced by the things of the world. Television, the Internet, school, relatives, and neighbors all pose a threat of exposing an innocent child to today's evils.

> This world brings only "change," it is never constant but in its disappointments. The world is but a great inn, where we are to stay a night or two, and be gone; what madness is it to set our heart upon our inn, as to forget our home!
>
> - *THOMAS WATSON*

While worldliness is to be avoided, we must reach the lost *in this world*. Christian schools, home schools and strong churches can indirectly cause our children to become isola-

While worldliness is to be avoided, we must reach the lost in this world.

tionists. If children do not see the lost men and women of this world as needing their Savior they can be tempted to covet their lifestyle. David cried to his friends, is there not a cause.(1 Samuel 17:29) Having a purpose, or cause, helps maintain proper focus of the world around us. Young people must unite in the great cause of reaching the world with the gospel message. Receiving a smallpox vaccination protects your from getting smallpox. A vaccination is actually a small amount of the disease, which guards you from getting the real thing. Having a small amount of Christianity can produce a similar result; never obtaining the real thing. Isolationism can inoculate a believer from becoming dedicated in service to the Lord. The Great Commission, as found in all four gospels and the book of Acts, commands believers to go into the whole world and preach the gospel. We must be careful to maintain a burden for the lost men and women of the world.

Establish a Family Altar

Since dad is the leader of the home, he should initiate meaningful devotions and a family altar. In those rare exceptions when dad is gone on business, working late, or experiencing a difficulty, his wife may lead the devotion time. However, Bible reading and prayer should be initiated by the father of the home. A family altar involves daily Bible reading and prayer with the entire family together. Although many creative suggestions for devotions are available, the basics of Bible reading and prayer must be understood to be the minimum activity. Finding a time—such as breakfast, dinner, or bedtime—is a good idea when planning the time you will have your family altar. Everyone should participate in some way, whether it is prayer, Scripture reading or providing some project or report. Family devotions need not be long, although there may be times when they are. At times devotions may become monotonous, but they should be conducted faithfully.

There is no secret to a family altar;
it only requires obedience.

Young children enjoy Bible stories; however stories should never be read to the exclusion of the Bible itself. As children become older they may take turns reading Scripture. Prayer could include each child, with dad and mom also taking their turn. Reading specific books of the Bible or specific topics of the Bible can be utilized. Our family memorized the Christmas story during our devotion time, and each Christmas we recite it together before we open our gifts. Verses specifically pertaining to children could be memorized: "Children, obey your parents in the Lord: for this is right. Honour thy father and mother; (which is the first commandment with a promise)" (Ephesians 6:1-2). Another verse we memorized was "Do all things without murmurings and disputings" (Philippians 2:14).

A weak family altar is better than no family altar and of course a good family altar is better than a bad one. There is no secret to a family altar; it only requires obedience. Reading the Bible and prayer may constitute the sum of your time, but having that time is priceless. Family devotions can sow the seed that one day will germinate into the salvation of your children's souls. Make your family devotions a habit and a wonderful time of blessing.

Loving Discipline

CHAPTER ELEVEN

Precious Memories

I was a typical mischievous boy. I know I was spanked several times and probably needed more correction than I received. However, two spankings stand out vividly in my mind. Once I remember being spanked right after taking my bath. To this day I do not know why I was disciplined, though I have no doubt I needed it. The other spanking stands out because I denied any guilt, even though I was indeed guilty. My sin involved using an ax to put holes though the covers of several homemade turkey feeders. My father had put considerable time and money into their construction, and my action ruined the feeders, requiring additional time and expense to repair them.

Though I lived on a small eighty-acre farm with one sister and no others siblings, I couldn't understand how my father discovered my guilt in this crime. (The closest children lived about one mile away, and my sister rarely ventured away from the house, so upon my fathers discovery of the vandalism it is understandable that he would make certain assumptions concerning who was responsible.) When my father asked if I had any knowledge about the holes in the feeders, I denied my crime. Knowing there were no witnesses to my awful deed I assumed there was no way he could possibly know I was the culprit. When I denied any knowledge of the incident he put me over his knee and spanked me. After the spanking he asked me again if I knew anything about the damaged feeders, which I again denied, hoping he would believe me. He spanked me soundly again and questioned me about my involvement. I still couldn't understand why he suspected me. Finally, I reluctantly admitted my sin and, mercifully, the spanking ended. I am thankful to have a father who took the time to teach me a very valuable lesson I never have forgotten. My father understood the importance of changing my spirit.

DO YOU REALLY LOVE YOUR CHILD?

> "He that spareth his rod hateth his son: but he that loveth him chasteneth him betimes" (Proverbs 13:24).

It is difficult for some people to see a relationship between the words *love* and *discipline*. However, the two words (and concepts) are inseparable in child rearing. Parents can and must discipline their children in love. The Bible explicitly states that parents who withhold correction from their children do not love them. The word translated hate literally means "to be an enemy." Failure to correct a child identifies a parent as unloving. It is important to understand the difference between beating a child and employing loving discipline. Chastening a child is proof of love, while refraining from discipline illustrates a lack of love. I have met my share of rebels and many times watched them destroy their lives. Rebellion has led fine, innocent young people on a downward path to drugs, drunkenness, promiscuity, disease, incarceration, and even premature death. I have performed the funerals services

---

Chastening a child is proof of love, while refraining from discipline illustrates a lack of love.

---

of rebellious teens who never received proper discipline to restrain their behavior. One young man at one time felt called to preach the gospel until his rebellion derailed his plans. I will never forget going to the scene of his motorcycle accident and mourning over his lifeless body. It was difficult to go to his home and explain to his mother that he was dead. Unfortunately, his sad story is not uncommon.

Small children need parents to protect them from dangers without, as well as within. Left to themselves small children can succumb to dangerous situations. Our granddaughter was born with a life-threatening stomach problem, yet she is constantly putting things in her mouth that don't belong there. When we see her chewing, we must force open her mouth and find out what she is eating. Little boys don't realize that knives cut and fire burns, often they must find out the hard way. After experiencing the pain of fire and the pain of an incision they begin to learn to become more responsible, but parents must realize their duty to constantly watch their children to protect them from danger. Failure to protect a child from physical harm could brand a parent as negligent, but if a parent fails to protect a child from social, emotional, and spiritual ills, he is especially negligent of his child. Heartache and tragedy can be turned into a blessing, as illustrated by Glen Cunningham. Glen was seriously burned and crippled while trying to light the old fashioned school stove. As a result, Glen was told he would never walk. Not only did he walk, but he won an Olympic gold medal for the mile. Glen's inspirational story is one of courage and triumph, but I have observed many other young people who never recuperated from their mistakes.

THE PURPOSE OF CHASTENING

The purpose of chastisement is to correct behavior. Correction should not be punitive, but corrective. Any form of discipline must have as its goal a change in the child's wrong behavior. Correcting wrong behavior is a difficult and time-consuming task, but it is very essential. Implementing godly discipline must be done in a biblical manner.

Wrong discipline methods

Spanking can be performed in a loving and firm manner, but it must not be done in frustration or anger. Properly disciplining a child requires a great deal of time and will involve teaching, restraint, affection, assurance, prayer, and acceptance. Simply hitting a child out of anger misses the opportunity of teaching and correcting him. The real purposes of spanking and discipline are to correct behavior and teach restraint. A child who has been properly chastened will learn to restrain himself, which is the real purpose of discipline. Shaming a child uses guilt to emotionally pressure him to obey. Telling a child you are ashamed of him does not teach him proper behavior, nor does it encourage him to obey from the heart. Shaming coerces a child to stop being an inconvenience or

---

Hitting a child out of frustration or anger is not godly discipline and should be avoided.

---

embarrassment. Shaming is nothing more than rejecting a child and withholding emotional approval, which can cause the child to disassociate from his family's love.

An unfortunate, but common disciplining technique is yelling or screaming at the offending child. Yelling is an immediate response to a wrong behavior, expressing disdain for the behavior, but also for trying to help the child deal with it. Sometimes yelling is accompanied by hitting. Hitting a child out of frustration or anger is not godly discipline and should be avoided. Wise parents should admit their past failings, reestablish a proper procedure of discipline and assure their child of their commitment to follow God's Word in this manner.

Dealing with a child's problems superficially is never a good idea. Consider the child's root problem in order to determine the best way to produce the right results. Grounding a child or withholding toys from him never really gets to the root of the problem, in fact restraining a child results in him not facing his sin and dealing with it. Discipline should deal with the true heart issues. Sending a child to his room may be easy, but it fails to teach the child any lessons from his infraction, and it fails to instruct him in how to face and correct his problem. If a child fails to finish his chores, the best way to teach him is to supervise him and insure he finishes the job. He doesn't belong in his room; he needs to learn to complete his duties. Supervision requires more effort initially, but in the end it corrects the behavior so that ultimately the child's behavior is changed.

Finishing an important task prior to enjoying a hobby teaches discipline, however punishing a child by arbitrarily restricting his activities doesn't teach a child right behavior, instead it alienates him from his parents. I have known parents who, unfortunately, restricted children from attending youth activities because they disobeyed. Punishing a child by restricting her from a spiritually challenging activity conveys the wrong message. Virtuous and good things should never be used as a form of punishment; doing so will cause the child to associate church and, ultimately, God with punishment.

Communicate with your Child

Communication involves speaking and listening. Listening to your children enables you to understand their emotions and needs, which is essential to loving discipline. A wise parent will try to fully understand all of the circumstances when a child has done something wrong, and then will employ appropriate discipline, based on facts. When approaching an offending child ask questions to get his response and force him to consider what he has done. Ask if he understands why his behavior was wrong. If he really doesn't know why he was wrong, give him a clear explanation of his error, impressing on him that now he will be responsible and held accountable if this occurs again. Express your disappointment and state that you know he is capable of better behavior. Direct your communication toward the Lord. The child must understand he has offended God and needs to make things right with Him. Be clear about how he must correct his offense. Explain the procedure of forgiveness and restoration. Explain what he should have done and what he must do next time. Explain the importance of your role and that you must obey the Lord because it is your responsibility to train him properly.

The explanation of rules and their enforcement can be outlined as follows:

1. Tell them what to do.
2. Tell them what will happen if they don't do it.
3. Review points one and two.
4. Follow through.

Children must learn to obey immediately, without complaint and with a pleasant spirit. No parent should continually warn a child punishment is coming. Warning should be given, and upon disobedience punishment must come. Don't threaten a child with something you cannot enforce. Idle threats breed bad habits. As a parent, you are responsible to honor the Lord and perform discipline in a way that is pleasing to Him.

Should You Spank Your Children?

The Bible clearly teaches parents to spank or chasten their children. Objections to God's plan of chastening range from human reasoning to fear. Our current society, with its humanistic philosophy, objects to spanking, stating it does not work

The purpose of chastisement is to nurture and admonish children.

and it is abusive to the child. Parents who don't discipline their children often lack courage, fearing their children will be alienated from them. Sometimes parents fear the disapproval of family and friends. But the Bible explains we must fear God. Unfortunately, we live in a day when every parent must be careful to avoid public spanking. Being reported to the police for child abuse is an unfortunate reality in our society; therefore proper discipline should be done in private. The purpose of chastisement is to nurture and admonish children. The word nurture literally means *the chastening of the Lord.* The word admonition means instruction. The Bible teaches parents to chasten and instruct their children to obey from the heart. "And, ye fathers, provoke not your children to wrath: but bring them up in the nurture and admonition of the Lord" (Ephesians 6:4).

> "And ye have forgotten the exhortation which speaketh unto you as unto children, My son, despise not thou

> the chastening of the Lord, nor faint when thou art rebuked of him: For whom the Lord loveth he chasteneth, and scourgeth every son whom he receiveth. If ye endure chastening, God dealeth with you as with sons; for what son is he whom the father chasteneth not? But if ye be without chastisement, whereof all are partakers, then are ye bastards, and not sons. Furthermore we have had fathers of our flesh which corrected us, and we gave them reverence: shall we not much rather be in subjection unto the Father of spirits, and live? For they verily for a few days chastened us after their own pleasure; but he for our profit, that we might be partakers of his holiness. Now no chastening for the present seemeth to be joyous, but grievous: nevertheless afterward it yieldeth the peaceable fruit of righteousness unto them which are exercised thereby." (Hebrews 12:5-11)

The Bible is our authority for faith and practice, and it is authoritative when it teaches us principles of child rearing. Read and meditate on the following Scripture passages:

- Proverbs 3:11 "My son, despise not the chastening of the LORD; neither be weary of his correction."
- Proverbs 13:24 "He that spareth his rod hateth his son: but he that loveth him chasteneth him betimes."
- Proverbs 19:18 "Chasten thy son while there is hope, and let not thy soul spare for his crying."
- Proverbs 20:30 "The blueness of a wound cleanseth away evil: so do stripes the inward parts of the belly."

- Proverbs 22:6 "Train up a child in the way he should go: and when he is old, he will not depart from it."
- Proverbs 22:15 "Foolishness is bound in the heart of a child; but the rod of correction shall drive it far from him."
- Proverbs 23:13-14 "Withhold not correction from the child: for if thou beatest him with the rod, he shall not die. Thou shalt beat him with the rod, and shalt deliver his soul from hell."
- Proverbs 29:15 "The rod and reproof give wisdom: but a child left to himself bringeth his mother to shame."
- Proverbs 29:17 "Correct thy son, and he shall give thee rest; yea, he shall give delight unto thy soul."

WHEN SHOULD YOU SPANK YOUR CHILDREN?

The Bible indicates discipline must begin early in life. Small children usually lack discernment. Rational thinking, as well as the ability to calculate and rationalize situations is beyond their ability. Because of this, children need parents to watch over them and help make decisions for them. Children may not understand your reasoning, but they understand the pain from a spanking. There is no exact age to begin spanking. But the Bible says it should begin early: "Chasten thy son while there is hope, and let not thy soul spare for his crying" (Proverbs 19:18). "While there is hope" indicates molding of character is still possible.

"He that spareth his rod hateth his son: but he that loveth him chasteneth him betimes" (Proverbs 13:24). The word "betimes" means early. When a child is able to respond to chastening it should be employed. I recall, the well-known evangelist Dr. John R. Rice saying a girl should be paddled six months after birth, but with boys you should begin immediately upon bringing them home from the hospital. He was joking, but I know he encouraged parents to begin discipline well before their first birthday. Spanking an infant should not be done with the same force as with a junior age child. Initially a small swat may be all that is necessary. As a child matures discipline should become less frequent, but more forceful. If a child laughs about being spanked he hasn't been spanked hard enough or long enough or both. The earlier a consistent plan of discipline is initiated the more rapid the effect in the child's life. Waiting until the teen years is too late. When a child becomes a teen he or she has become a young man or a young woman, old enough for self-discipline. Self-disciplined teenagers should require little or no spanking. Molding a child's character with outward discipline will establish an environment in which he is able to discipline himself. Child training is teaching a child through instruction, repetition, and discipline.

HOW SHOULD YOU SPANK YOUR CHILDREN?

1. Agree together
2. Never spank in anger
3. Don't wait until you blow your top

4. Always keep your promise
5. Don't spank in front of other people
6. Don't slap or hit in the face
7. Don't spank without telling them why
8. Never give them more than two warnings
9. Do it slowly and deliberately
10. After you spank them ask them if they will do it again
11. Be sure they do not sob too long after you are finished
12. Always hug them and tell them you love them
13. Pray with them

Whenever my wife or I spanked one of our children it was usually a long and involved process. We did not spank our children for every misdeed. Spanking was relegated to serious or persistent evils. Some deeds automatically deserved a spanking, while at other times spanking was a result of a continued infraction. Every parent must determine what misbehavior and what severity of infractions will be punished. As an example, for our children, we considered lying to be a much more serious than failure to brush their teeth. I would rather my children have a cavity than become a criminal. Of course I would rather neither happen, but the spanking was reserved for the greater offense. The strictest discipline must be exercised as little as possible, thus making its effect of greater consequence.

If you decide spanking is necessary, then the next question is how to do it properly. My wife and I began with a time of questioning: *What did you do? Was this wrong? Why did you do it? Do you know what the Bible says concerning this matter? The Bible teaches that this is a sin, and as your parent I must chasten you; if I fail to chasten you I will have sinned. Do you realize I am disappointed in your behavior? Your mother is disappointed and the Lord is disappointed. I love you very much and I expect more from you. I know you are capable of the right behavior.* After I considered all the facts, including their remorse or lack of it, I determined an appropriate plan of action, which I explained to them in detail. The result may be one small swat on the bottom, two, five or more.

Our procedure continued by turning them over my knee. I would have them stand between my legs and bend the over one knee. Depending on their age the method may have to be

---

A strong-willed child may require more discipline than a more passive child.

---

altered slightly. While very young I used a polo paddle that had lost the ball from the rubber band (similar to a ping-pong paddle). As the children became older I used a more substantial paddle. I placed my hand behind their head, bent them over my knee and gave them the number of swats promised. After spanking them I sat them on my lap and reviewed the entire process again: *What did you do that was wrong? Why did you do it? Will you repeat this again? I know you are capable of doing better and that is what I expect from you.* I always would hug them and pray with them at the end of the session. After the entire process was complete I would tell them how much I loved them and that I would be praying that God would help them to do right. This process could take ten minutes to half an hour, but it always required stopping my immediate tasks and concentrating on my child.

Sometimes everything did not go smoothly. With young children you may need to remove or lower their diaper. Older children may require a different technique to hold them down. Sometimes children will repeat the same offense almost immediately. A strong-willed child may require more discipline than a more passive child. There is a limit to how much and how hard a child should be disciplined. Common sense and reason must be exercised. A child unaffected by your discipline may require a more harsh spanking, while a passive child may not require as much. The Bible indicates spanking is severe enough to cause tears from the pain (don't spare them for their crying). I can personally attest to the difficultly of observing my children's tears during this experience. There have been times my wife and I both had tears from this process. However it is much better for the tears to be early in the child's life, before the tears are from a serious sin later. "He that spareth his rod hateth his son: but he that loveth him chasteneth him betimes" (Proverbs 13:24).

Not every mistake or every sin needs to be punished by spanking. The Bible indicates spanking should be early in the child's life. An older child may require more severe spanking, but if he has been spanked early in his life seldom will it be required later. You may question what other method of discipline you can employ besides spanking. Talking to them is the most important form of discipline available. But don't just lecture; explain and present the ramifications for future infractions. Also, every parent must consider the age of their children and what they are capable of doing. No child should be punished for something they cannot avoid. Little children will spill their milk and for that matter sometimes parents do too. It is expected.

TEACH YOUR CHILDREN

Teach them to respond to you. The first matter of discipline for children should be teaching them to come to you. I have observed parents chase their child, while the child knows he is disobeying their commands. Disobedience is not a laughing matter, and it is never cute. A disobedient child could run into traffic and be killed simply because no one taught her to respond to authority. Every child must learn the meaning of NO. Children should learn respect, good manners, and consideration for others. All children will experience sibling rivalry and these opportunities can be utilized to teach character. I remember on one such occasion my children were arguing over something, at times they enjoyed needling one another. I finally decided they would stand together, facing each other and not move until they resolved their conflict. I didn't know who started the argument or who was at fault, but I explained they must resolve the issue before they could move. To this day I don't know what they did, but after only a few minutes they did resolve the problem. The point is that our goal should be to help our children correct their behavior and make right decisions on their own, realizing we will not be with them forever.

While my youngest daughter, Sarah, and I were visiting a missionary in Japan we all decided to do some shopping at a local mall. I remember a child screaming and throwing a temper tantrum, which could be heard throughout the entire mall. The missionary explained to me that very few members of this culture spank their children and further explained that the child's parents would try to reason with him. Eventually we came upon the family, observing the child lying on the

Appropriate discipline requires consistency, persistence, and self-control.

floor, attended by the parents stooping over him, and trying to reason with him. The screaming persisted the entire time we shopped. I felt like offering my services to fix this problem, but of course it was not my place to do so. Unfortunately, this family knew nothing of Biblical discipline.

"And thou shalt teach them diligently unto thy children, and shalt talk of them when thou sittest in thine house, and when thou walkest by the way, and when thou liest down, and when thou risest up" (Deuteronomy 6:7). We must constantly monitor and guard our children's behavior. Appropriate discipline requires consistency, persistence, and self-control. Rearing children is a tough business and not for the faint of heart. If you think your children will rear themselves you are mistaken. The responsibilities of parenting require diligence twenty-four hours a day, seven days a week. The rod teaches children to honor parents, while the parents provide children with clear limits to safeguard their well-being. Spanking demonstrates love and yields peace and good fruit. A child will be blessed who has been raised under proper discipline. Discipline will create security, respect, and a close bond between a child and his parents. Though chastening is not a pleasant experience, it must be done with the future in view. There will be wonderful results that one day will bring gratification, knowing you followed the exhortation of God's Word: "Now no chastening for the present seemeth to be joyous, but grievous: nevertheless afterward it yieldeth the peaceable fruit of righteousness unto them which are exercised thereby" (Hebrews 12:11).

Responsible Independence

CHAPTER TWELVE

Precious Memories

Farm life offered a daily opportunity for teaching responsibility. Work was a way of life, for adults and children. I have never considered myself as abused because I was expected to work on the farm; in fact, I consider those who didn't have such responsibilities as having been deprived. A strong work ethic and a sense of responsibility are invaluable character traits sadly missing in much of today's society.

As a young child my father taught me to drive a John Deere tractor, a chore I still love. While I drove, Dad stood behind me on the drawbar, offering me suggestions and correcting my mistakes. When he deemed me capable, he taught me how to plow, cultivate, and plant. He carefully orchestrated every step to achieve his goal of teaching me to perform all of these tasks on my own—and he succeeded. Even before my teen years I had learned to plow a straight furrow, put up hay, plant, cultivate, and harvest corn. As I reflect on those early life experiences I understand the purpose of my father's training. He wanted me to learn responsibility even more than he desired a good harvest.

Most people would be surprised with their children's ability if they encouraged and taught them to assume responsibility. Unlike farm life, rearing my children in a pastor's home required inventing ways to teach them. One thing I found helpful in their training was mowing our lawn and the church lawn. We couldn't afford a fancy lawnmower so we purchased an old Wheel Horse garden tractor. That mower had to be repaired every time we mowed. I remember the boys offering suggestions (complaining) about the poor condition of this piece of junk. I coined a cliché to repeat to them. I said, "You boys are receiving free training, for which most people have to pay. You are fortunate because you are receiving it for free." They would roll their eyes and return to repairing that lawnmower. We probably could have afforded something better, but that tractor became a tool to teach my boys responsibility. Eventually we did purchase a much better lawnmower, after they both had enrolled in college.

AUTONOMOUS CHILDREN

Another possible title to this chapter could be "autonomous children." Preachers often use the word autonomous when speaking about church planting or missions, indicating every new church eventually should become self-supporting and self-governing. Just as a church should become self–supporting, our children also should become self-supporting and self-governing. I've often said there is only one thing worse than having your children grow up and leave home, and that is for your children to grow up and not leave home. One day your children will probably leave the confines of your home, but the question will be, are they ready?

A controlled environment offers the opportunity for children to face challenges monitored by their parents. Allowing children the freedom of failure in controlled circumstances is far better than helplessly standing by and watching them later suffer dire consequences for wrong decisions. No child will ever achieve maturity without making mistakes. Protecting children from all failure does great harm, because we learn our greatest lessons through failure. The key to teaching responsibility is to offer the right opportunities at the right time. It would be improper to allow a drug dealer access to your child. However you might want to allow a neighborhood friend who doesn't share your beliefs to have some contact with your child, to help your child learn that not everyone believes the same things you believe. Monitoring such a situation may offer an opportunity to teach your child why your beliefs are superior and should be followed. Our oldest son developed a friendship with another Christian boy who didn't live by the same principles we live by. After visiting this boy's home a few times our son realized some serious problems existed in that boy's home. Several positive conversations developed from that experience that helped form some important decisions in our son's life.

Facing adversity, and even failure, can provide necessary character lessons. In high school I played on a basketball team that had a losing record. Losing is never fun, and this was no exception. As I look back on that experience I realize how many learning experiences it provided. Among other things, I learned humility, the importance of teamwork, and distaste for failure. Wise parents will provide the right opportunities so that their children's mistakes will build character and not destroy them.

RESPONSIBILITY MUST BE TAUGHT

"Don't do that! You can't have that! I said no!" Phrases such as these are necessary to teach restraint and discipline and are essential to training children. However, the "don'ts" and warnings are only half of the equation. Teaching character involves more than restricting children from danger. By the time children reach maturity they must learn to make decisions for themselves. Someday your teen will ask to go somewhere, see someone, or do something that will require sound judgment. Generally, parents are given eighteen years to prepare their

---

By the time children reach maturity they must learn to make decisions for themselves.

---

children for that moment. The process of good decision-making involves learning through years of experience. Wise parents who understand this will take advantage of opportunities early in their children's lives, when they can control the decision-making situations. At the point of a child's birth his parents should have the foresight to realize that someday this infant will be making decisions about college, marriage, an occupation, friends, music, church, etc.

Only after becoming a parent did I recognize that many of the things my father taught me were things he knew would benefit me. Following my father's lead, I decided I needed to think of ways I could teach my children responsibility in controlled environments. Learning honesty, hard work, frugality, endurance, and strength are all benefits of this type of learning. Every child must learn that life is full of limits. Many young people have ruined their lives because they followed the wrong crowd and participated in the wrong things. Parents must accept the responsibility of training and monitoring every detail of their children's lives. Choosing the right friends is extremely important, as is proper etiquette, proper dress, and pleasant speech. Children are dependent on their parents for guidance, because they lack the life experiences that parents have gained. Lessons concerning responsibility will instill character in a child. "Train up a child in the way he should go: and when he is old, he will not depart from it" (Proverbs 22:6).

"Honey, keep junior away while I try to fix the faucet." "Honey keep little Sally out of the kitchen while I try to prepare dinner." Perhaps you have made similar statements. Children can get in the way, and at times certain activities are inappropriate for them. Similarly, children can make some tasks more difficult, so we tend to remove them from the activity to make our life easier. The question that must be asked is, "When do we train children?" Must there be a classroom situation before they can learn, or can children learn from life's everyday activities? I'm reminded of the science teacher who called the children in from recess and reminded Johnny that he must return the frog to the pond and come to science class immediately. The teacher missed the opportunity to teach through everyday life situations. Little boys can learn to hold the wrenches for their dad and to be a helper while he works. Children can be an annoyance, and they make life more difficult, but we must utilize these daily opportunities to teach them. Baking cookies can be a messy task, and involving small children can make a huge mess. But, again the parent's job is to involve the child and teach her to not be messy. This type of teaching makes life more difficult, but the opportunities to allow your children the privilege of making mistakes under your watchful eye provides the opportunity to correct them while they are gaining confidence in learning the task. Recently my two oldest grandchildren and I decided to make an apple pie. When we finished, flour and sugar were everywhere and the kitchen was a mess, but we all had a great time. They are not yet prepared to bake on their own, but they did learn a little bit of responsibility. The pie tasted great, but unfortunately my wife's slice contained a piece of plastic that somehow was sneaked into the apples.

Many years ago a teenage boy was informed his father was moving out of the house and seeking a divorce form his mother. Such news is tragic to anyone, and especially to a teenager. To my surprise the teen's only response was, "Dad isn't taking the TV with him, is he?" Unfortunately, this father had largely ignored his child. I recall another couple who complained they couldn't discipline their child because he had no interest in anything so they had nothing to take away from him. Evidently, the child's only activity was to move from the TV to the refrigerator. Parents must encourage children from an early age to find good and wholesome interests. Music, sports, hunting, fishing, landscaping, gardening, reading, art, and many other hobbies are all necessary for the child to learn and enjoy. Although children possess few abilities at birth, parents who are willing to take the time can train them to become proficient and helpful.

How do you find tasks to help train children about responsibility? You can have them clean their room and take out the trash, but that's not enough. Try to determine your child's interests and build on them. Just because you liked sports doesn't mean all of your children will love sports. You may be studious, but your child may be more vocational. Some children are task-oriented and some are people-oriented. As a parent you must learn your children's personalities and interests. Everyone must learn to clean their room and do their homework, but not everyone will enjoy playing the violin or learning woodworking. Observe your children while they're young and begin to discern their interests. If a child has musical ability, perhaps music lessons are in order. If the child responds well to the lessons, then continue those lessons. If a child enjoys sports, then provide opportunities for them to participate in a controlled environment. A child's positive interests should be encouraged and directed. Training should include observing role models. I remember my father pointing out to me a basketball player I should emulate. My father taught me to be generous by giving me fifty cents right before the offering and then telling me I could do whatever I wanted with the money. I felt proud to place that money in the offering. I knew I was pleasing my parents, and of course the Lord, by doing so. Too often these situations never occur, because a parents' control is so overwhelming a child never is allowed to make a decision. Parents must provide opportunities to learn how to handle money, deal with people, face obstacles and even how to deal with failure.

WHAT DO YOU WANT TO BE WHEN YOU GROW UP?

Children should be taught to seek a virtuous profession. Becoming a bartender, model, or movie star is not something to which a Christian should aspire. There are many honorable professions, but youth should seek their highest

Children should be taught to seek a virtuous profession.

calling in order to please the Lord. Books and learning are extremely important; however without wisdom knowledge will come to naught. Encourage your children to love books and to learn new things, but be certain they know how to apply knowledge.

Today's society notoriously lives for money, fame, and fortune. Most teens preparing to enter college or the workforce are focused on material things. Sometimes kids never think beyond having a car and attending parties with their friends. By the time these teens near thirty they still have no savings and no ambition; they will have played the fool. They may fall into drug addiction, alcoholism, and/or promiscuity, which will lead only to destruction. "The devil is seeking whom he may devour and these pleasure seekers are easy prey. Be sober, be vigilant; because your adversary the devil, as a roaring lion, walketh about, seeking whom he may devour" (1 Peter 5:8).

Parents should encourage their children to seek God's best. Discovering God's will and living by faith are invaluable lessons. Young girls should keep themselves pure for their prospective husband, and young men should do the same for their future wife. Contentment should become their goal. A factory worker, a secretary, a teacher, or a preacher all typify professions that serve the community, require effort and represent a respectable profession. Serving in any of these capacities or others like them, in the context of a dedicated Christian, is worthy. Young people should place in their room a sign that boldly states, Not for sale, I'm seeking God's best for my life. "But godliness with contentment is great gain" (1 Timothy 6:6).

If It Doesn't Kill You It Makes You Stronger

I am not suggesting parents jeopardize their children's safety. Every loving parent should seek to protect their child from danger. However, we can also succumb to the hidden danger of overprotection. Children get dirty, make mistakes, get hurt, and suffer the consequences of their mistakes. Too much pampering is detrimental to their well-being. Little boys should learn to walk like a man and talk like a man. Little girls must learn to act like a lady, talk like a lady, and walk like a lady. Cleaning house, cooking, and homemaking are duties girls need to know how to perform. Boys need to realize the high cost of providing for a family. They also need to learn to help with chores around the house. Every young man must learn how to work; to develop blisters and bruises. When it snows, dad should teach junior how to shovel the snow. I remember the time my cousin drained the transmission from his father's car and added five quarts of oil to the engine. It was a costly mistake, and my cousin never repeated it. The time required to teach basic skills is well worth the effort.

The story of Abraham Lincoln is a testimony of a man learning from failure until he achieved the highest office in the land, President of the United States. Mr. Lincoln was born into a family of no fame or fortune. When Abe was nine, his mother died, so he was raised by his stepmother. As an adult, Lincoln ran for Congress and lost. The village store he worked in went out of business. Lincoln and his partner, William Berry, purchased another village store in New Salem. That store also failed, leaving Lincoln in deep debt. Then, when William Berry died, Lincoln's debt rose to $1,000 (a heavy financial burden for that time.) Ann Rutledge, a young woman whom Lincoln loved and admired, died from a fever, though later he did marry. Then Lincoln lost another election for Congress, and soon after his son Edward died. Then Lincoln lost an election for the Illinois legislature. Finally (and providentially), in 1860 Abraham Lincoln was elected as America's 16th president (and the first Republican). Abraham Lincoln's trials contributed to his greatness. We must not fear struggle; it will strengthen us.

Teenager Is Not A Disease

Chapter Thirteen

Precious Memories

I have always loved being with teenagers. When I was a child I worked on the farm with teenagers, and I thoroughly enjoyed it. As a teenager I enjoyed my peers. When I was a young church planter our church consisted of teenagers who just happened to bring their parents. In fact we would have had very few members had it not been for our teens. As a parent I enjoyed my children's teen years the most. Now, as an older pastor, I still love to be around teenagers and minister to them. Each one of our children learned to serve the Lord with us. It was with great joy that my wife and I watched our children mature, develop ministry skills, and become blessings to others. The two boys learned landscaping, building, and bus ministry, while the girls learned to clean the church and play the piano, as well as planting flowers and shrubs.

For a brief time all four of our children were in their teen years. Our home was busy with them constantly coming and going. They had music lessons, sports, school and church activities, and church ministries. Now I must admit I miss the noise they made and the disturbance they created. I believe a preacher's home was a great place for our children to grow up. We have always counted it a privilege to serve the Lord, and our children have sensed our commitment. There are some challenges growing up in a preacher's home, but the blessings far outweigh any negatives.

Activities I especially enjoyed with my teenagers were special missions trips. I took each of my children to at least two mission fields. These trips were costly, but invaluable. Each child learned to appreciate America and also learned to have compassion for others. These trips offered a special time of bonding. Elizabeth and I were in Paris in the springtime. Jonathan and I camped overnight on an island off Costa Rica. David and I visited a banana plantation in Brazil. Sarah and I learned how to eat rice and fish in Japan. All the memories these trips created have been stored forever in their minds, and I hope in some way these times have made them better Christians. I thank God for teenagers.

I Love Teenagers

What kind of person would love teenagers? Aren't the teen years to be feared and endured? When children have been trained at an early age, the teen years can be a wonderful experience. I still miss those years. Teens enjoy activity, and there are so many things they can do. They should be able to accept responsibility and accomplish tasks in an adult manner. At the adolescent stage teens are learning to develop heartfelt beliefs and convictions. What a blessing to be a part of their maturing process.

We cannot force teenagers to obey as if they are small children. Many teens retain an element of childhood mischievousness, but at the same most of them begin to want adult privileges and responsibilities. Teens may challenge your decisions, and sometimes for good reason, but I always greeted these challenges as opportunities for them to learn. Sure, they didn't always fit into my preconceived "box," and at times their challenges caused me to expend extra time and effort to help them, but I enjoyed the process of watching them learn and I never felt intimidated by their questions. I always saw these challenges as part of their learning process.

There is a time for questions and a time not to ask questions, and parents must distinguish between the two. Sometimes parents simply need to say, "You must do this because I am responsible for you and you are responsible to obey me." Some questions don't deserve an answer, and sometimes teens should obey simply because you said so. Parents who learn to explain the right answers at the proper time will earn their children's respect, so they can say, "Because I said so," and the child knows you have a good reason. Perhaps I am different from most parents, but I still love teenagers, and not just my own. I can't wait until my grandchildren are teenagers.

Teenagers Possess a Powerful Resource

Teens often receive undue criticism for being teens. Adults often expect teens to act like adults when they are not adults.

Being a teen is not an excuse for obnoxious behavior, but teens need opportunities to gain experience, and those opportunities may include some failures. Infants do not learn to walk the first time they try, and teens will not act as responsibly as they should all of the time. Training your children is an ongoing process, and it does not end at sixteen. I have seen too many

---

Training your children is an ongoing process, and it does not end at sixteen.

---

parents abdicate their parenting responsibilities because their child has reached age sixteen. Celebrating a birthday does not qualify a youth to make all their decisions and be their own boss. If they live in your home, eat your food, and ride in your car, then they must answer to you.

Proverbs chapter seven reveals some important challenges concerning the struggles of youth. In the teen years, attraction to the opposite sex becomes a powerful instinct. Physical attraction of the opposite gender is God-given, and it goes all the way back to the Garden of Eden. God provided for Adam by giving him Eve. The woman was a perfect fit for the man. Adam and Eve fulfilled one another's needs. But in teens, these powerful, new emotions must be understood and controlled.

The teen years afford a wonderful opportunity for parents to teach children the proper philosophy of marriage. Through presenting the right model in your marriage and teaching Biblical principles of marriage, teens will form a godly paradigm of their future home. Christian parents must be prepared to help their children through these new challenges of becoming an adult. Proverbs seven gives a graphic and sad picture of the failure in an ungodly society, and we should help teens learn from it.

Strongholds Of The Past

The Bible speaks of the sins of the fathers being passed on to children unto the third and fourth generation, but positive traits also can be passed along to children, grandchildren, and great grandchildren. Tremendous effort is required to break

---

The teen years are formative times when behavior patterns often are established for the future.

---

the bondage of the sins of the past, but with the Lord's help it can be done. Not everyone has a strong Christian background when they call on Jesus as their Savior, and the lifestyle of past generations can continue to hinder future growth. Receiving Christ is a transforming influence and will produce changes for every new believer, but some sins of the past may stubbornly grip Christians for some time. However, change is possible as we learn to die to self and walk in the Spirit. The teen years are formative times when behavior patterns often are established for the future. Overcoming these sins of the past may require years of struggle, thus it is better to form right behavioral patterns during these teens years. The goal of being like Christ should never waver. Realizing the old man must die and the new man must be strengthened, we learn to mortify the body. If past sins grip your life you should learn the meaning of Paul's admonition to the church at Colosse. "Mortify therefore your members which are upon the earth; fornication, uncleanness, inordinate affection, evil concupiscence, and covetousness, which is idolatry" (Colossians 3:5). Mortify means to deny or abstain from.

Mortification keeps sin from depriving us of power and peace. Every unmortified sin will certainly do two things:

1. It will weaken the soul, depriving it of its life.
2. It will darken the soul, depriving it of peace.

Many lose their way during their teen years. Drugs, promiscuity and violence are but a few of the vices destroying teen lives. Scars can remain a lifetime, even well after a rebel has returned home and found forgiveness. Teens can become alcoholics or drug addicts, and suicide is all too common. Depression and fear can grip young lives and destroy their happiness. Overcoming addictions and sins of the past can be a difficult challenge. I would rather protect and prevent children from sinful practices and instill character in their lives, instead of confusion. But, if a teen loses his way, it is important to realize there is hope in Christ.

Salvation is of the Lord, and He will forgive and save to the uttermost. Salvation is offered to all who will come. The Lord will change the lives of those who turn to Him for salvation and forgiveness. The scars can last a lifetime, but the Lord can provide forgiveness and reconciliation. No one should commit sin to receive grace, but where sin abounds grace does much more abound. Our sins humble us to remind us of our need of a Savior, and for this we can be grateful.

TEENAGE REBELLION

Rebellion doesn't germinate in one day; it develops over a long time. A teen with a rebellious heart is like a time bomb ticking away and waiting to explode. Problems that have developed over many years continue to build until one day they explode. A single incident may trigger the outward rebellion, but many problems will have contributed to the problem over several months or years.

Rebellion doesn't germinate in one day; it develops over a long time.

Outward rebellion is a result of parents allowing inward rebellion to germinate. Parents who admit their shortcomings and failures in properly nurturing their rebellious children increase the prospects for positive results. Blaming others will result in continual problems. No one wants to accept blame for their teen's actions, but failure to accept responsibility only masks the opportunity to help cure it. "Train up a child in the way he should go: and when he is old, he will not depart from it" (Proverbs 22:6).

Common reasons for teenage rebellion are as follows:

1. *Lack of restraint*
   Well-meaning parents who give their children everything they desire pave the way for trouble. "For I have told him that I will judge his house for ever

for the iniquity which he knoweth; because his sons made themselves vile, and he restrained them not" (1 Samuel 3:13).

Eli failed with his own children, while Samuel became one of the godliest men ever to live. What was the difference between them? By the time Hannah presented Samuel to Eli in the temple she had already taught him restraint. Every child must learn the meaning of no! No one should receive everything his flesh desires. The specifics of Eli's failure are not detailed, but I can imagine that he did not use the rod, as Proverbs prescribes, and he must have allowed his son's sins to go unpunished. In addition, because of his position as High Priest, these boys could have almost anything they wanted, which Eli seemed glad to give them. The Bible explains Eli honored his sons above the Lord (1 Samuel 2:29) while Hannah dedicated her son Samuel to the Lord (1 Samuel 1:28). The contrast of these two homes is very revealing. Giving a child everything he wants, while refusing to implement discipline, is a recipe for heartache.

2. *Lack of parental involvement*
   "The rod and reproof give wisdom: but a child left to himself bringeth his mother to shame" (Proverbs 29:15). Parents must not ignore children's emotional and spiritual needs. Children need parents to guide them as they mature in life. Taking a child fishing, working on a project or teaching them to help others

are all important lessons that parents must accept as their responsibility in childrearing. Taking an active role in the child's life by attending games, recitals, meetings, and many other activities is a crucial aspect of parenting. Consider this important truth: A well-respected father who expresses interest in his daughter will rear a confident young lady who will not need to find approval and affection from someone outside the home.

3. *Wrong friends*

   "Ye adulterers and adulteresses, know ye not that the friendship of the world is enmity with God? Whosoever therefore will be a friend of the world is the enemy of God" (James 4:4). "He that walketh with wise men shall be wise: but a companion of fools shall be destroyed" (Proverbs 13:20). "Be not deceived: evil communications corrupt good manners" (1 Corinthians 15:33).

   Parents should closely monitor their children's friendships. Developing the wrong relationships can adversely affect a child's behavior. Great care should be taken concerning relationships at school, college, clubs, sports teams, and relatives. There are only three choices concerning your children's friends: (1) Remove your children from all contact with the world. (2) Allow your children contact with the world indiscriminately. (3) Teach your children to stand on their own and become a positive influence on the world. We must be reminded that Israel's greatest failures were two extremes: (1) Learning the ways of the world. (2) Not making the Lord's name known to the world. Removing your children completely from the world misses the responsibility to go into the world and make God's name known. The point is a child needs to stand on his own, while also being a good testimony.

4. *Provoked by the actions of parents*
   Parents' sin will be evidenced in their children's lives. A sinful lifestyle is inexcusable for parents. Yet, often children grow up not knowing where their parents are during the day or at night. I once conducted a poll to determine if parents knew where their children were. To my surprise I found most children were home, but they didn't know where their parents were. Swearing, screaming, drugs, alcohol, and immorality will scar a child's mind. Parents must be role models for their children. A child who never knows who her mother will bring home overnight will suffer mightily. As parents, we are role models—for good or bad.

What not to do when a child becomes rebellious

1. *Don't, don't, don't defend their sin.*
   When a young person is disobedient, their sin must not be defended. Don't fear your child will not like you. Your children don't need you as a friend; they can always find friends; they need you to be a par-

ent and tell them they are wrong and their behavior is unacceptable. Defending sin is a big mistake, especially when you are responsible to teach your child to do right. Today's trend encourages parents to go to the teacher when they are reprimanded and complain that the teacher is singling out your child. Many reading this may find it hard to believe, but the culture of the sixties and before would never find a parent siding against a teacher or any authoritative person. Forty years ago, public schools taught kids to respect their parents, their leaders, and their country. That's not always the case now.

2. *Don't diminish your dedication to the Lord.*
   "Don't get too involved serving the Lord, because you could lose your own children," I was told. Nonsense! A dedicated Christian has a much better opportunity of passing on a godly heritage than a marginally involved Christian. However, constantly being at church while your children are neglected is not being a dedicated Christian. Families are wise to serve the Lord with their children. Our children planted flowers, mowed lawns, cleaned the church, worked on a bus route, and helped construct several buildings. The Lord's work became their life. Sorry to say, many parents come to a work day at church and leave their children at home. These folks are missing a golden opportunity to teach their children to serve the Lord.

3. *Don't change churches to get your child to go with you.*
   (If the church is the problem, you should prayerfully consider finding a fundamental church that upholds family ideals.) Disobedient children might plead they will attend another church if their parents will go with them, so the parents mistakenly give in to their pleas and leave their home church. Teenagers can quickly learn how to manipulate their parents and cause havoc in the family. Leaving a church you love in order to please your child will do nothing to change your child for the better.

4. *Don't ostracize them.*
   Abandoning your own flesh and blood is inexcusable. Even if your children are in serious trouble they need to be reassured of your love for them. You can hate their sin while still loving them. Every possible way you can find to express your love without participating in or encouraging their sin should be employed.

5. *Don't blame someone else for their rebellion.*
   It is easy to blame your ex-spouse or the lack of a second parent in the home as the reason for your child's bad behavior. The lack of a second dedicated parent may contribute to a child's delinquency, but it is rarely the single reason for it. Your children's friends also are an easy target of the blame game. Face the facts that your child is rebellious and determine to do something about it. Accept your part in their failure and determine to make the necessary changes in your own life.

6. *Don't lower your convictions.*
   Rules should be based on wise decisions and should never be changed as a compromise to accommodate a rebel. Changing personal standards will be of little assistance in changing your child's heart. His problem is a heart problem and needs to be settled in his heart. Rules that are without any Biblical basis and of no practical value could and should be changed, but only if they serve no value. Otherwise, keep your rules the same and your standards high. "Hate the sin, love the sinner" is the catch-phrase we Christians so often use—and so many in the world hate—but it's true and wise. Tolerating cohabitation with another young person in your home is unwise. I have heard the argument, "They're doing it anyway, so it's better if done in my home." Sin should never be tolerated. Have the courage to stand up for what you believe and let your children know sin will not be tolerated in your home. What if they have nowhere to live? Your child can always repent and return to your loving care, which should be your goal.

7. *Don't ignore the problem.*
   A problem that is ignored only becomes worse. Ignoring obvious problems will not solve them, but facing them can solve them. Don't expect someone else to solve your problems. Determine to do whatever is required to bring your child back to the Lord.

What to do when your teen is rebellious.

1. *Search your heart.*
   Even though children are personally accountable for their actions, when they rebel, parents must also recognize how they may have contributed or allowed this rebellion to occur. Searching your own heart is always difficult. Sadly, in my teen years I rebelled, even though my parents were good people. My rebellion was causing friction in our home. However, my family had not been in church for several years and consequently I knew very little about the Bible. Oddly, I loved my parents very much, but after experiencing "freedom" in the world, the world's pull was greater than that of my family. The best thing that could happen did: My father and mother began praying continually for me. My mother reached a point where she couldn't eat because she was so overwhelmed with grief and discouragement. In spite of our conflicts, most people would have considered our home happy and perfectly normal. I'm thankful my parents could not accept my sin as normal. It was through their fasting and prayers that my life was turned around.

2. *Confess your sin and seek forgiveness.*
   Begin by asking forgiveness from God. You have not just failed yourself and your child, but you have failed your God. In addition, you should go to your teen and ask their forgiveness. They might think this

strange, but it is important to establish the fact that you are now seeking God as your ultimate authority.

3. *Humble yourself before the Lord; seek His intervention.*
   Ask God to show you where you have failed. Seek godly counsel to help you see where you can change

4. *Pray.*
   Pray daily for your child and, as necessary, your prayers should be accompanied with fasting.

5. *Witness to your children concerning their salvation.*
   Don't nag them, but lovingly let them know of your concern for their soul.

When will rebellion leave?

1. *Employing godly discipline can drive wickedness from a child's heart.*
   After a child becomes a teen, this is less likely to be effective. "Foolishness is bound in the heart of a child; but the rod of correction shall drive it far from him" (Proverbs 22:15).

2. *When a sinner comes to the end of his way.*
   I don't wish anything bad on a rebellious child, but sometimes hitting bottom is the only thing that will get their attention. "And when he had spent all, there arose a mighty famine in that land; and he began to be in want" (Luke 15:14).

3. *After time has passed to reveal their error.*
   Keep the door open for your child to return to you. If you close the door it may hinder his confession of sin and repentance. "And when he came to himself, he said, How many hired servants of my father's have bread enough and to spare, and I perish with hunger!" (Luke 15:17).

Not only is rebellion a serious offense against a Holy God, but a teen may die in his rebellion. Unfortunately, history reveals many young people have suffered severe consequences for their sin. The seriousness of rebellion is well expressed by the adage, "Sin will take you farther than you want to go, keep you longer than you want to stay, and cost you more than you want to pay." Rebellion should never be taken lightly.

- "Be not deceived; God is not mocked: for whatsoever a man soweth, that shall he also reap. For he that soweth to his flesh shall of the flesh reap corruption; but he that soweth to the Spirit shall of the Spirit reap life everlasting" (Galatians 6:7-8).

- David, the man after God's own heart cried and mourned over the sin and death of his son Absalom: "But the king covered his face, and the king cried with a loud voice, O my son Absalom, O Absalom, my son, my son!" (2 Samuel 19:4).

Rebellious actions, such as drug use and gang involvement, are like playing with fire. You never know when you will be burned and scarred for life. The very first funeral I conducted as a young pastor was for a teenage girl who had become involved with drugs. Her body was crushed when she fell from a mountain. I have been to accident scenes, hospitals, courtrooms, and even the funeral homes to witness the sad results of rebellion. No one should underestimate the severe consequences of childhood rebellion. A shortened life is a very real possibility for a rebel. The first commandment with promise (from the book of Exodus) is repeated in the book of Ephesians. "Honour thy father and mother; (which is the first commandment with promise) That it may be well with thee, and thou mayest live long on the earth." (Ephesians 6:2, 3)

A Special Note on the Rebellion of Pastors' Children

I recall my college basketball coach mentioning in a sermon how he wished he had been reared in a pastor's home. It seems his home was a pleasant place to live, but, generally, the expectation of children from a pastor's home is higher than that of others. The expectations should be higher; however, the failures of a few need not represent the many whose children are faithfully serving the Lord with a good heart. I have observed many of my friends whose children have grown to love and serve the Lord. Unfortunately, there are exceptions in which preachers' children have rebelled and become points of contention in churches. Commitment to full Christian service is no guarantee your children will follow, so you must apply the Scripture truths that will ensure your children's loyalty to the Lord. Pastors' homes do have special challenges other families may not face, such as being in the spotlight, lack of finances, frequent moves, and poor treatment by other church members. There are special challenges, but there are advantages as well. Though we had limited funds, our children never felt we were poor, in fact they were afforded opportunities other children were not afforded. Your situation is always what you make it and we have chosen to be thankful for the blessings.

The Fourth Generation

Chapter Fourteen

Precious Memories

While doing some research on my family genealogy I discovered some amazing facts. My parents and grandparents were very good people, and for good reason. Strong spiritual roots were developed through the influence a Baptist preacher/farmer named Henry Moody. My mother was a direct descendent of Mr. Moody, and my great-grandmother on my father's side of the family also was a direct descendent.

Only recently I have gained a new appreciation of my lineage. My father's parents always had an interest in helping young men get started in the ministry. Though we attended a small country church, my grandfather felt the church served a special purpose as a training ground for young men to preach the gospel.

As a young man, the last thing on my young mind was becoming a preacher, yet my grandparents prayed for one of their decedents to serve the Lord in that capacity. It seemed unlikely my grandparents' desire would be fulfilled when the church closed due to a lack of members. As a result of the church closing, my family strayed from the Lord. My teen years were filled with selfish desires and living for the world. However, my parents' and grandparents' prayers followed me. Through a period of repentance and prayer, the Lord brought my family back. Just before my nineteenth birthday, I became a Christian and surrendered to the ministry.

Shortly before his death, my grandfather received an answer to prayer when I stood before him and preached the Word of God. He did not live to see the full effect of his prayers, because through a late-in-life baby, my parents produced another son who today is a missionary. In addition, my two sons both are preachers, faithfully serving in the ministry, and my older daughter recently married a preacher who is an assistant pastor and making plans to start a new church. My younger daughter is seriously dating a young man who is surrendered to preach the gospel. Influenced by a preacher named Henry Moody, my grandparents prayed for a preacher in their family. God answered their prayers.

I don't know the extent of my future influence, but I do know a man named Henry Moody had a godly influence through eight generations. I pray that I may have similar influence on future generations of my family, even those not yet born.

THE CHILDREN OF LOT

Lot's home was the antithesis of a godly Christian home and, unfortunately, an example of what not to do. The Bible states that Lot was a just man. Apart from that statement we would never know he was a believer. Poor decisions affected his marriage and children.

Lot's wrong decisions are well chronicled for us in the book of Genesis:

- *He looked* toward Sodom, longing for the worldly things it offered.
- *He leaned* toward Sodom daily, tempted by its allure.
- *He lusted* for its riches and material goods.
- *He lived* in Sodom, following a wicked lifestyle.
- *He lingered* so long that he lost his family and reputation.
- *He lost* his family, friends, neighbors, and all his possessions.
- *He left* Sodom with only his two unmarried daughters. His wife and the rest of his family perished in the fire and brimstone God cast on Sodom.

> "And delivered just Lot, vexed with the filthy conversation of the wicked: (For that righteous man dwelling among them, in seeing and hearing, vexed his righteous soul from day to day with their unlawful deeds)" (2 Peter 2:7-8).

> "Likewise also as it was in the days of Lot; they did eat, they drank, they bought, they sold, they planted, they builded; But the same day that Lot went out of Sodom it rained fire and brimstone from heaven, and destroyed them all" (Luke 17:28-29).

THE FOURTH GENERATION

Every generation has the choice of leaving a godly heritage or an evil one. There is an amazing correlation between the sins of the parents and the sins of the children. Also, the converse is true: Godly homes beget godly children. The same mistakes frequently are passed on from one generation to another. Christians must realize the importance of breaking the bonds of their parents' sin by allowing the Holy Spirit to deliver them from the shackles of the past. No one need commit

---

Every generation has the choice of leaving a godly heritage or an evil one.

---

the same sins as their parents, but without the Lord's help we are apt to do just that. Notice the many Scriptures that verify the plight of many homes that seem doomed to the mistakes of a previous generation. "Thou shalt not bow down thyself to them, nor serve them: for I the LORD thy God am a jealous God, visiting the iniquity of the fathers upon the children unto the third and fourth generation of them that hate me" (Exodus 20:5).

- *A generation blinded by their sin*
  "There is a generation that curseth their father, and doth not bless their mother. There is a generation that are pure in their own eyes, and yet is not washed from their filthiness. There is a generation, O how lofty are their eyes! and their eyelids are lifted

up. There is a generation, whose teeth are as swords, and their jaw teeth as knives, to devour the poor from off the earth, and the needy from among men" (Proverbs 30:11-14).

- *A generation that is evil*
  "Hear this, ye old men, and give ear, all ye inhabitants of the land. Hath this been in your days, or even in the days of your fathers? Tell ye your children of it, and let your children tell their children, and their children another generation" (Joel 1:2, 3).

- *A faithless generation*
  "He answereth him, and saith, O faithless generation, how long shall I be with you? how long shall I suffer you?" (Mark 9:19).

Good or evil can be passed on to the third and even the fourth generation. Decisions today will influence tomorrow

---

Good or evil can be passed on to the third and even the fourth generation.

---

because our children and even our grandchildren will be affected by our choices. Consider the prophetic statements of Scripture in this regard:

- "Thou shalt not bow down thyself unto them, nor serve them: for I the LORD thy God am a jealous

God, visiting the iniquity of the fathers upon the children unto the *third and fourth generation* of them that hate me" (Deuteronomy 5:9).

- "And the LORD said unto Jehu, Because thou hast done well in executing that which is right in mine eyes, and hast done unto the house of Ahab according to all that was in mine heart, thy children of the *fourth generation* shall sit on the throne of Israel" (2 Kings 10:30).

- "This was the word of the LORD which he spake unto Jehu, saying, Thy sons shall sit on the throne of Israel unto the *fourth generation*. And so it came to pass" (2 Kings 15:12).

While meditating on these verses I was challenged to consider my legacy. I asked myself what I wanted for my children and my children's children. My wife and I tried to begin with the end in mind. We tried to create a clear picture of our objectives in child rearing. I recall while viewing my first child through the glass of an incubator that I prayed for his salvation. Our desire for was for him to be saved and serve the Lord. As his parents, our vision for his life included a Christian marriage, consecrated service, and a surrendered spirit. It was my desire that each of my children belong to the right kind of church. After I leave this earth to meet my Savior, my desire for my children is to continue to follow the "Old Paths" that have been proven. The following list is guidelines for determining a good church in which to belong.

1. *A church that teaches a clear salvation message.* I want the best for my children, and I don't want them to have to decipher a complex sermon to understand the Bible's clear teaching on salvation. My desire is that they will always be faithful to a church where the clear plan of salvation is preached without fear or compromise. Three teachings will be evident in such a church.
   a. The fundamentals of faith will be preached.
   b. The salvation message will emphasize assurance of salvation.
   c. The evidence of salvation will result in a changed life.

"Neither is there salvation in any other: for there is none other name under heaven given among men, whereby we must be saved" (Acts 4:12).

2. *A Church that preaches repentance from sin.* When churches lower their standards they always trim their message of repentance. The conditions to salvation are repentance and faith. No one can be saved without both. A fundamental church will be known for its preaching on sin.
   a. *Preach on sin* (all sin), including backsliding.
   b. *Preach on revival.* The spirit of revival should burn consistently in a good church. It is a shame that so many members grow up in a church that has never had a hint of revival. I pray my descendants will guard against this tragedy.

c. *Leaders who hold high standards of separation from worldliness.* Music, dress, and entertainment all will change with the newest fad, but godly people will never be swayed.

"And be not conformed to this world: but be ye transformed by the renewing of your mind, that ye may prove what is that good, and acceptable, and perfect, will of God" (Romans 12:2).

"Love not the world, neither the things that are in the world. If any man love the world, the love of the Father is not in him. For all that is in the world, the lust of the flesh, and the lust of the eyes, and the pride of life, is not of the Father, but is of the world. And the world passeth away, and the lust thereof: but he that doeth the will of God abideth for ever" (1 John 2:15-17).

"Ye adulterers and adulteresses, know ye not that the friendship of the world is enmity with God? whosoever therefore will be a friend of the world is the enemy of God" (James 4:4).

3. *A Church that emphasizes the family.* Family values should be prominent in a good church.
   a. *Character is born in home.* Andrew Murray of South Africa raised eleven children to adult life. Five of the sons became ministers and four of the daughters became minister's wives. The next generation saw ten grandsons become preachers

and thirteen became missionaries. The secret to this ministry was the Christian home.

b. *Worship together as a family.* Families should attend church together, sit together and pray together.
c. *Godly virtues must be exalted.* "A virtuous woman is a crown to her husband: but she that maketh ashamed is as rottenness in his bones" (Proverbs 12:4). "Who can find a virtuous woman? for her price is far above rubies" (Proverbs 31:10).

4. *A church with godly leaders*
   a. *Deacons, teachers, and soul-winners who are good model of Christianity.*
      What America needs is a leader like Moses who refused to be called the son of Pharaoh's daughter, an army general like Joshua, a food administrator like Joseph, a preacher like Peter, a mother like Hannah, a child like Samuel, a physician like Luke, a God like Israel's, and a Savior like Jesus!
   b. *Men and women of vision and sacrifice.*
   c. *Members who exhibit faith in God.*

Aim at nothing and we are bound to hit it. Rearing children is not like spinning the wheel of fortune. Training children to live for God is more choice than chance. From an early age, begin with the end in mind. What do you want them to be? Once you envision your child as an adult, consider the necessary steps to help them realize their highest potential.

CREATING A LEGACY

As defined in the *American Heritage Dictionary*, a legacy is: "Something handed down from an ancestor or a predecessor or from the past." Often a legacy is some object or material good, but a Christian legacy is passing down a godly heritage.

I remember, as a teen, talking to my grandfather about continuing our family name. I knew it was of great importance to him as he had instilled this desire in my life. My grandfather was wise to consider the importance of a godly heritage. Years ago it was common for parents to remind their children to be careful not to bring reproach on their good name. In small communities it could indeed impair the reputation of a family if only one member brought reproach upon it. Unfortunately, today's society doesn't place the same value on a good name.

Valentine Wightman bears a remarkable legacy of faith. His grandfather was Edward Wightman, the last Christian martyr burned at the stake in England in 1612. In 1705 Valentine planted the First Baptist Church in the state of Connecticut, located in Groton. He served as pastor there for forty-two years. Pastor Wightman's son, Timothy, succeeded his father and pastored the church forty more years. Timothy's son, John Gano Wightman, continued as pastor another forty years. The Wightman family pastored the First Baptist Church more than 120 years. In addition, Valentine Wightman's youngest son, John Wightman, became a preacher and started the first Baptist church in Southington, the town where I serve. At least five generations of preachers continued to preach the gospel, even though it was a time of limited tolerance. The character of this family is evident for all to observe. The Wightman family was not lucky, they were godly and dedicated.

FAMILY TRADITIONS AND LASTING MEMORIES

Consider the history of the word, "heirloom." Women of the past not only made clothes for the family, they even made the cloth to make the clothes. They spun the wool and then wove it into cloth, using a loom. This loom was of great importance to a family's survival and often resided in the center

Daily family devotions are heirlooms that should be an established tradition of every Christian family.

of the house. As time passed, this loom would be passed on to one of the family heirs, thus the term heirloom. The inheritance of a good name and godly character bears a similar resemblance as the heirloom that will ultimately prove to be of greater value.

Daily family devotions are *heirlooms* that should be an established tradition of every Christian family. Daily family Bible reading should an instilled memory for every child. Memorizing Scripture can provide a lifetime of encouragement and blessing. My family memorized the Christmas story, and yearly we recite it before we open our presents. Special holidays, birthdays, and special occasions offer opportunities to establish wonderful traditions for your family. Vacations and family trips offer a special time, with lasting impressions. These traditions provide a sense of belonging and well-being that are essential to the maturing process.

When my wife and I moved to Connecticut we stayed four days with a wonderful Christian family while we were looking for an apartment to rent. Each day we observed the wife as she prayed with each of her four children before they left for school. She also took the liberty to pray with us before we started our day. Her godly example provided a pattern we followed with our children.

Living a thousand miles from your birth family presents special challenges, but we developed a tradition of spending two weeks with them every summer. At our reunions we enjoyed fishing, swimming, Fourth of July parades, and more. These times provided opportunities for our children to get to know their grandparents and to identify with our roots. Everyone always looked forward to these special days, and they have provided many special memories.

I enjoyed hunting and fishing with my sons and special times with my daughters. We now treasure those special memories. Playing golf in the back yard was just as much fun as playing at the golf course. Piano and music lessons provided an opportunity to teach our children excellence, hard work, and practice. We not only had fun playing together, we even learned to enjoy working together. Every church project became a family project.

One day your children will look back to their childhood either with remorse or thankfulness. Parents can provide traditions and memories that will be reflected upon with satisfaction. My childhood days on the farm provided me with a multitude of experiences that today I greatly cherish. Fun things like fishing, mushroom hunting, sports, bicycling, and exploring were accompanied by tending the animals, plowing, planting, haying, building, and numerous other tasks. All of these experiences developed my frame of reference. Your children's experiences will provide their frame of reference. Leaving a child to himself will mean his paradigm is formed by strangers, and probably not by godly influences. You must take advantage of every opportunity to provide a godly heritage for your children.

"The memory of the just is blessed: but the name of the wicked shall rot" (Proverbs 10:7). "And this day shall be unto you for a memorial; and ye shall keep it a feast to the LORD throughout your generations…" (Exodus 12:14). This passage talks of a memory, or memorial maker, and is tied to eating, a church tradition in itself!

Feasting was a biblical custom the Old Testament Jews practiced several times a year. Exodus 23:14 states, "Three times thou shalt keep a feast unto me in the year." Although we don't have the sacrifices and trips to the temple that the children of Israel had to make, we too have at least three times a year that we as Christians have "feasts": Easter, Thanksgiving, and Christmas.

The Bible even explains who to include in the feasts: Deuteronomy 16:14 says, "Thou shalt rejoice in thy feast, thou, and thy son, and thy daughter, and thy manservant, and thy maidservant, and the Levite, the stranger, and the fatherless, and the widow, that are within thy gates." In other words, open your doors. Have your family in, and have those that have no family. Are you willing to open your house to others who may not be as fortunate as you?

Weddings, funerals, birthdays, graduations, reunions, and births are examples of events that call for tradition to set our pattern of observance. Many times a wedding rehearsal is accompanied with the words, "This is tradition." Although your wedding traditions may differ from others' traditions, both probably have strong opinions as to what is important in a wedding. The same could be said of funerals, birthdays, and several others special occasions. Take advantage of special days and develop some good traditions for your family.

THE FAMILY OF GOD

Every Christian family must recognize the importance of their relationship to their local church. The Bible teaches that Christians are members of a body. This is true not only of individuals, but also of the entire family. Submitting to the

---

Every family must recognize the importance of its relationship to the greater good of the church.

---

authority of the local church is a safeguard with immeasurable value. Every family must recognize the importance of its relationship to the greater good of the church. It is sad when parents speak in negative terms about other church members. Children who hear such negative talk will soon lose respect for the church and eventually for their parents. In Paul's letter to the Corinthian church he carefully explained the importance of every member for the good of the whole body (1 Corinthians 12:12-27). Other Scripture passages suggest the church is similar to a family by stating that the older women should teach the younger women and the older men teach the young men. Healthy members have a responsibility to help those that are sick and weak. Members of a church assembly are called brothers and sisters in Christ, terms of family endearment. A Christian family always has an extended family that is often as close as their blood relatives. This phenomenon has been evident to me on mission trips. Though I can't speak the language of the people I'm visiting, our shared love for the Lord bonds us.

- "And we beseech you, brethren, to know them which labour among you, and are over you in the Lord, and admonish you; And to esteem them very highly in love for their work's sake. And be at peace among yourselves. Now we exhort you, brethren, warn them that are unruly, comfort the feebleminded, support the weak, be patient toward all men. See that none render evil for evil unto any man; but ever follow that which is good, both among yourselves, and to all men. Rejoice evermore. Pray without ceasing. In every thing give thanks: for this is the will of God in Christ Jesus concerning you. Quench not the Spirit. Despise not prophesyings. Prove all things; hold fast that which is good. Abstain from all appearance of evil. And the very God of peace sanctify you wholly; and I pray

God your whole spirit and soul and body be preserved blameless unto the coming of our Lord Jesus Christ." (1 Thessalonians 5:12-23)

- "And he answered them, saying, Who is my mother, or my brethren? And he looked round about on them which sat about him, and said, Behold my mother and my brethren! For whosoever shall do the will of God, the same is my brother, and my sister, and mother." (Mark 3:33-35)

- "And sent Timotheus, our brother, and minister of God, and our fellowlabourer in the gospel of Christ, to establish you, and to comfort you concerning your faith." (1 Thessalonians 3:2)

CONCLUSION

"Except the LORD build the house, they labour in vain that build it: except the LORD keep the city, the watchman waketh but in vain. It is vain for you to rise up early, to sit up late, to eat the bread of sorrows: for so he giveth his beloved sleep. Lo, children are an heritage of the LORD: and the fruit of the womb is his reward. As arrows are in the hand of a mighty man; so are children of the youth. Happy is the man that hath his quiver full of them: they shall not be ashamed, but they shall speak with the enemies in the gate." (Psalm 127:1-5)

This wonderful Psalm must be studied carefully, because building a home requires God's power. God ordained the home, and He values it greatly, thus we must never diminish the importance and the power of the home. Our homes must follow God's pattern if we are to be successful. We are weak and frail, but our God is great and powerful, thus we must put our faith in Him. If we fail, we must turn to our Savior, pleading for forgiveness and restoration. By acknowledging our failures we can be forgiven and renewed. Someday you will face some special challenges, and by trusting in the Lord He will help you to face them triumphantly. Always keep a godly perspective of hope. The future is as bright as God's promises. We live in an imperfect world, but we must learn to be thankful for what we have and not regret the meagerness of our belongings. Count your blessings and be thankful to the Lord. Thankfulness is a good way to begin building your home.

Christian homes must have Christ as their center. The salvation of every member is vitally important. The old hymn still challenges us today of the importance of reaching our loved ones with the gospel. I recall a sermon illustration by the late evangelist Fred Brown where he repeated the story of a mother's quest to see that all of her children were saved. I recall Dr. Brown's story as follows:

Following a stirring revival service a man named John asked to speak with me. He explained that he was raised by a godly mother and father, but unfortunately he and some of his family went through a time of teenage rebellion. "Late at night my brother Bill and I would return home after a night of revelry." Bill was always the last to return, and when his mother heard the screen door shut she would call out, "Bill you're the last one home, so close the latch." My mother continued to pray for our salvation, and one-by-one we all accepted Christ, except for Bill. "At her deathbed she asked me to promise to do everything in my power to encourage Bill to be saved." John explained, I literally followed him around the world to witness to him, and recently he trusted Christ as his

Savior. Brother Brown, when Bill and I get to heaven, do you know what I expect to hear my mother say? "You're the last ones home close the latch!"

This Welsh classic expresses the true attitude of a godly family:

"Guide me, O thou great Jehovah,
Pilgrim through this barren land;
I am weak, but thou art mighty;
Hold me with thy powerful hand;
Bread of heaven,
Feed me till I want no more."

APPENDICES

Appendix # 1: Family Rules

The following suggestions do not need to be displayed on your kitchen wall, but should be developed to help guide your children. When there are no guidelines, parents will find themselves making rules that have not been well developed. We had very specific rules, but the categories below are listed for you to develop as you deem helpful. Both parents should agree to the rules you determine, and these rules must be taught and developed with the child. Rules that are developed through prayer and counsel can easily be explained and defended through simple logic. Children should be taught the rules and the reasons for having them. Waiting for your children to come to you, seeking permission to date or use the car will one day surprise you unless you have taught them and prepared them with your philosophy earlier. I suggest parents take the time to pray and seek godly counsel to develop their own specifics for their rules.

CARS

- At what age should allow your children to get a driver's license?
- May they use the family car, and if so, under what conditions?
- Who will pay for the car, gasoline, and insurance?
- Will misuse of the car result in the loss of any privileges?
- Will there be restrictions on passengers, or sitting in parked cars, etc?

DATING

- The term dating is meant to include courtship and all terminology that could lead to marriage.
- Determine age requirements prior to developing a boy-girl relationship.
- Under what conditions can a relationship be developed?
- Should chaperones be required?
- When must a parent be notified about a relationship?
- Must parents approve of all dates?

TELEPHONE, INTERNET, and VIDEO GAMES

- Who may call whom?
- How long may children or teens talk on the phone?
- Is privacy allowed, or must calls be only where parents can hear?
- What kind of filter is used for the computer?
- May children use chat rooms?
- May they e-mail their friends?
- Is there password protection?

- May they have their own cell phone?
- May they have a television in their room?

CLOTHES and MAKE-UP
- Who has the final decision on clothing?
- May girls have their ears pierced, and if so, at what age?
- May girls wear make-up, and if so, at what age?
- What clothing and appearance guidelines should boys follow?
- May boys wear jewelry?

BABYSITTING
- Must mother or father approve all jobs?
- Will you allow friends to visit you while you are on a job?

CHORES
- Will responsibilities be required to be completed before any personal endeavors are undertaken?
- What chores will children be given in the home?
- Will you provide an allowance for your children? Will you pay your children for work done in the home?

MONEY
- Will you require a percentage of all money earned and received as gifts to be deposited in a savings account for future education?
- Will you require at least one-tenth of all money must be tithed to the local church?

- Will you provide freedom to allow the rest of their money to be spent as they wish?

CHURCH

- Will you allow hobbies or sports to conflict with church activities?
- Will you expect your children to sit with or in front of you at all services?
- Will you prohibit secular work that requires missing regular church services or functions?

APPENDIX # 2: THE DEVELOPMENT OF A GODLY CHILD

The contrast of a wise son and a fool (Proverbs 10:1-4)

- Four levels of character (Proverbs 1:1-7, 22)
  1. *Wise son* – One who follows God
  2. *Simple son* – One who is led easily either way
  3. *Scourner* – One who is a rebel against God
  4. *Fool* – One who has no hope

- How to develop a wise son (Proverbs 1)
  1. Teach them to listen to their parents. (Proverbs 1:8)
  2. Teach them to not listen to the unsaved. (Proverbs 1:10)
  3. Teach them to not make friends with the unrighteous. (Proverbs 1:15)
  4. Teach them to seek wisdom. (Proverbs 2:1-5) (Don't let them act like a know-it-all.)
  5. Teach them to obey rules from the heart. (Proverbs 3:1, 5-7, 9)
  6. Teach them to accept correction. (Proverbs 3:11)
  7. Teach them to be consistent every day (Proverbs 3:21)
     A. Do good to others
     B. Don't envy oppressors
  8. Teach them to discipline their life and keep their heart. (Proverbs 4:20, 23-27)
     A. Put away froward lips
     B. Set worthy goals

C. Know where you are headed
   1. Teach them moral purity. (Proverbs 5:1-3)
   2. Teach them to fulfill every promise. (Proverbs 6:1)
   3. Teach them to work. (Proverbs 6:6)
   4. Teach them to not be froward. (Proverbs 6:12)

- Seven things to guard against (Proverbs 6:16-19)
  1. Proud look
  2. Lying tongue
  3. Hurting the innocent
  4. Evil heart
  5. Quick to mischief
  6. False witness
  7. Sowing discord

- Parents must accept the responsibility of teaching

APPENDIX # 3: LORD, AS A SINGLE CHRISTIAN I CHOOSE...

1. To marry only a Christian. *(2 Corinthians 6:14)*

2. That God's goals for my life will be compatible with God's goals for my spouse's life, and I will help my spouse develop in his/her maturity in Christ. *(Amos 3:3; Colossians 1:28, 29)*

3. That my behavior with my future spouse will be on a par with God's accepted standards. *(1 Thessalonians 4:3–8; James 1:13–15)*

4. That our activities will honor and glorify the Lord. *(Colossians 3:17; 1 Corinthians 10:31)*

5. To realize that my date is God's property, and that He has the right to do with His property what He wants. *(Ezekiel 18:4; Romans 14:8)*

6. To concentrate on developing the qualities God wants to be a natural part in my life. *(Psalm 37:4: Matthew 6:33)*

7. To be willing to remain unmarried as long as the Lord desires. *(1 Corinthians 7:7–9)*

8. When our conversation becomes serious about engagement and marriage, to discuss our intended plans with each other's parents.

9. Not to marry without the full consent of both sets of parents. *(Ephesians 6:1-3)*

10. To be sensitive to God's timing for marriage, with due consideration given to financial stability. *(Ephesians 5:28, 29)*

APPENDIX # 4
IDEAS TO ENHANCE YOUR MARRIAGE

Remember special days

- Anniversaries
- Birthdays
- Valentines Day
- Christmas
- Easter
- Mothers Day
- Fathers Day
- Thanksgiving

Have a date every week

- Eat out
- Go shopping
- Go sightseeing
- Walk together
- Play a game at home
- Fix popcorn and sit in front of the fire
- Go on a boat ride
- Enjoy hobbies together
- Invite another couple over

Sweet words

- I love you
- I'm sorry; I was wrong
- Compliment daily homemaking
- Compliment daily provisions
- You're attractive to me
- Encouragement

Nice surprises

- Flowers
- Gifts
- Notes
- Unexpected phone calls
- Jewelry
- Cards
- Candy
- Ice cream
- Perfume
- Something unusual and spontaneous

Five things a man should do for his wife

- Every husband should date his wife at least once a week.
- Every husband should spend some time with his wife every day.
- Every husband should lead his wife in the work of the Lord.
- Every husband should lead the prayer life of his home.
- Every husband should solicit ideas and suggestions from his wife.

APPENDIX # 5
GOALS FOR TEENAGERS

- Make the Lord first place in your life
- Maintain a pure heart
- Seek Biblical wisdom
- Learn the fear of the Lord
- Honor your parents
- Learn the value of submission to authority
- Rejoice in the Lord
- Develop a close personal walk with the Lord
- Become a dependable person
- Learn to stand alone
- Learn how to get along with other people
- Gain victory over the flesh
- Keep yourself pure
- Live by faith
- Know you are saved
- Practice good financial stewardship
- Become a godly leader
- Experience the power of prayer
- Memorize Scripture
- Develop a skill
- Know how to work
- Enjoy hobbies that have value
- Learn to enjoy good music
- Visit the sick and elderly

- Lay aside the sins and weights that beset you
- Become a student of the Bible
- Develop proper etiquette
- Develop good study habits
- Be involved in the ministries of your local church
- Learn to prefer others first

APPENDIX # 6
FAMILY TRADITIONS

What are some things you can do as a family, on a traditional basis that will build memories. Allow me to suggest some ideas.

- Pick some special foods that you "always" have: Pies, sandwiches, soup, etc.
- Set aside some specific scripture that you "always" read
- Schedule game time or activity time that you "always" do: Puzzles, monopoly, etc.
- Sing as a family
- Visit neighbors
- Sing Carols to your neighbors
- Call specific friends/family
- Put up special decorations
- Get dressed up
- Treat your guests to special privileges
- Tell stories
- Cook together
- Take naps
- Watch special videos
- Do special things (basketball with the kids, bowling, ice skating/roller blading)
- Play special music; get out those "old" tapes and CDs
- Visit the police headquarters, firehouse, hospital, and drop off some goodies
- Check on the local military staff that might have "duty" - Visit their barracks
- Labeling of Christmas gifts